Kate Lawrence provides us with a clear, insightful guide for simple living. If you sincerely work to follow this guide you will find that you are in fact actualizing your best nature of selflessness and compassion, liberating yourself from isolation and sorrow. Words are cheap but the transformative PRACTICE of simple living is divine, bringing peace to one's self and the world.—**Ven. Danan Henry Roshi,** Spiritual Director, Zen Center of Denver

This lovely little book is a thoughtful exploration of the barriers to living a life of contentment and satisfaction. Kate Lawrence offers a rich palette of practical peacemaking suggestions based on principles of non-harming, care for others, and commitment to an ethical path. Drawing from her own personal efforts, she shows how practicing peace and compassion can be the true basis for healthy people and communities, and thus a healthy world. Though obstacles are endless, Kate Lawrence convincingly invites us to take up the path of peace in the midst of everyday life, to generate harmony within ourselves as well as among our friends and family.—**Stephanie Kaza,** author of *Mindfully Green*, Professor of Environmental Studies, University of Vermont

Walking our talk is the key to the future. Reading *The Practical Peacemaker* is the best guide to saving the earth as we know it.—**Howard Lyman,** author of *Mad Cowboy*

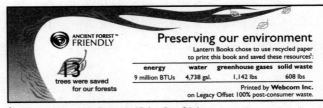

The Practical Peacemaker

How Simple Living Makes Peace Possible

Kate Lawrence

Lantern Books · New York

A Division of Booklight, Inc.

2009
LANTERN BOOKS
128 Second Place
Brooklyn, NY 11231
www.lanternbooks.com

Printed in Canada

LIBRARY OF CONGRESS CATALOGING-IN-PUBLICATION DATA

Lawrence, Kate.
 The practical peacemaker : how simple living makes peace possible / Kate Lawrence.
     p. cm.
 ISBN-13: 978-1-59056-140-9 (alk. paper)
 ISBN-10: 1-59056-140-6 (alk. paper)
 1. Lifestyles—Economic aspects. 2. Advertising. 3. Environmental degradation. 4. Consumption (Economics) I. Title.
 HQ2042.L39 2009
 361.2'5—dc22
                         20080455

In loving memory of my parents, Delmer and Ruby Cook. Over thirty years after their deaths, my dad's strong sense of ethics and my mom's everyday concern for others permeate these pages.

⌐ Table of Contents ⌐

~ Acknowledgments ~

I wish to acknowledge:

All my ancestors, teachers, and mentors for persevering through difficult times in order to pass along their precious gifts of life and wisdom;

Dr. Bonnie Benda, for her thoughtful reading of the manuscript and helpful suggestions;

And especially Keith Akers, the love of my life, for unreservedly supporting all my efforts, and for saying "You ought to write a book" so many times that I finally did.

Simple Living Makes Peace Possible

When we read or listen to the news, we encounter horror stories every day. We hear of agonizing violence between nations, between groups within one nation, within cities and families, and even within one person that causes heartbreaking suffering for thousands. We hear of terrorists sacrificing their lives in order to kill many others. We see that greed all around us and the fragmentation of society is leading to poverty, loneliness, and despair. Often we feel powerless—what can we possibly do?

Many of us want to do something to help, to raise our voices against the violence. We wish for peace, pray and meditate for peace, sing and dance and walk and march for peace, write letters, attend seminars and workshops, stand in protest demonstrations or silent vigils for peace. We may encourage international exchange work to hasten peace, and may wear or display peace slogans on T-shirts or bumper stickers. I have done these things and would not want to discourage people from these kinds of activism. Such action may inspire or plant a kind thought momentarily in someone's mind, b ut it is not enough. The next moment that person's mind is distracted and on to something else.

The truth we need to realize and begin to act upon is this: No matter how fervently expressed, words or wishes alone—whether in prayer or politics or on protest placards—will not bring the results we long for. As Mahatma Gandhi said, we must be the change we want to see in the world, and it must happen consistently and on a broad scale. So long as we live wastefully, which in effect treats other people and the planet arrogantly, and we ourselves are too time-stressed and mentally scattered to be peaceful ourselves, we continue to negate the peace we say we want. As in all things, we need to begin with ourselves.

This book is intended to describe the activism of changing our own habits, outlining what we can do that really *can* make a difference, especially if groups of us decide to pursue these changes together. We must make a demonstration or silent vigil of our very lives, and show others by example how to live in simpler, more conscious ways. Authors of earlier books about simple living have pointed out what such a lifestyle will do for us personally in increasing our life satisfaction, or what it will do for the environment. We'll review some of those arguments in these pages, but we urgently need to broaden our vision. Simple living is not only for ourselves and our planet's resources, but a way to make more food available; to reduce war, terrorism, crime, domestic violence, and debt; to address the ravages of overpopulation; to reverse the skyrocketing rates of obesity, heart disease, cancer and other Western diseases; and to restore sanity to our society as a whole.

Simple living does more for world peace than being nice to one's neighbors can ever do. Although friendliness is important, I believe even a cantankerous curmudgeon does far more for peace, if he lives frugally, than does a kind and politically active person who is profligate with resources, setting an example of callousness and waste.

It's true that the simple living practices of limiting our possessions and focusing our awareness can bring *us* peace as well. When I have traveled in the Global South (third world), I have been amazed at how much joy some of the poorest people exhibit. They live reverently, strong in their families and in their sense of place. They work hard but are rarely in a hurry, and are unpretentious and friendly to strangers. Some suffer from malnutrition and disease and/or live in the midst of wars, and so cannot be said to be living peaceful lives. Seeing them, I find myself thinking that if they just had access to basic health care, enough money to adequately support their families, and freedom from living in a war zone, they would have what they need to live in peace. Most of us in the U.S. can obtain health care, have more than enough money to meet our needs, and do not live in the midst of armed conflict, yet surveys show we are not happy. There is no reason why we cannot relearn qualities of a simpler, more peaceful life.

As we'll see in the following pages, obstacles to peace may arise from the personal choices we make, over which we can have considerable control, or from corporate or societal forces, over which we may feel we have little control. As we examine each of these, we'll see how simple living can effectively address them all. The despair and paralysis we may feel in the face of the human selfishness and conflict all around us can be greatly alleviated by the realization that simple living is something we personally can do, without waiting for others to change, and *it works*.

I hope you will join with those who have already caught the vision of simple living as a concrete and practical answer to creating a more peaceful world. You always have a choice. You can retreat into cynicism or apathy and resist changing your habits, adopting the view that world events are in an inevitable downward spiral beyond anyone's control. You can decide you are able to remain unaffected by such events. Or you can make one small change after another, even if you are not always consistent, knowing that you are trying, and that how you live matters.

If you make the latter choice, may this book help guide your way.

The Three Aspects of Simple Living

At least a shopping cart full of books about simple living have been written over the last couple of decades, and hundreds of specific suggestions have been made. To avoid any confusion before we go further, we need to clarify what we mean by simple living as we'll be using it in this book.

Simple living as a practical pathway to peace has three aspects. First of all, it is the conscious commitment to *using the least of the earth's resources we can* while still being comfortable and having enough. Simple living is not about deprivation and denial because as we limit our material goods, we find our lives enriched in other ways. Those ways may include the option of working fewer hours because our expenses have decreased, a reduction of the time and energy spent on insuring and maintaining lots of "toys," or better health from eating more vegetarian meals. What is required to be materially comfortable will be defined differently by each of us, but I believe that people sincere about being practical peacemakers will learn to distinguish the essential from the excess.

Essential expenditures in this context are not limited to food, housing, clothing and basic transportation, but could include tuition to further one's education, art supplies or athletic equipment, or thoughtfully planned entertainment and travel. What's important is to keep asking ourselves questions about minimizing environmental resources. The basic questions to ask include: *Can I do what I want to do in a different way that will be less consumptive of resources? Can I be happy doing an energy-intensive activity less often? Does what I think makes me happy really make me happy?* Activities that are notoriously heavy users of energy are transportation, especially driving alone in a fuel-inefficient vehicle, having large families (except by adoption), heating and cooling a poorly insulated home, eating meat, and buying new and imported items.

Getting down to specifics, we might ask more questions: *When I want to go to restaurants, classes or movies, can I bike or take public transportation instead of driving? Do I own a fuel-efficient vehicle? For my vacation, can I explore destinations closer to my home, or, if going farther, can I travel to one place and stay there for the duration of the trip? In the case of getting certification or training for career advancement, can I meet requirements through online courses rather than commuting to a classroom building? For clothing and furniture, can I get the desired items in good used condition at consignment or thrift stores or at yard sales, rather than buying them new? Instead of stopping every morning for a latte (made from coffee shipped from South America), can I cut back to once a week? Is the latte truly conducive to my happiness, or is it a source of unwanted weight gain?*

Secondly, simple living means *limiting our time commitments*. Are we rushed all day long from one task or appointment to another, falling farther behind on deadlines, feeling we have to forego activities we truly enjoy? A stressful lifestyle is inimical to peace within ourselves, and thus to peace in the world. Everyone needs "down time" for both mental and physical health, and must be proactive in setting aside time for it. Time spent doing nothing is not wasted, but may accommodate a prayer or meditation practice, lead to useful problem-solving insights, help us be better prepared for activities later in the day, or allow a refreshing nap. We can create needed space in our schedules by asking these questions about proposed activities: *Do I really want to do this or will I wish I hadn't agreed to it? Can I do this and still have time to do what I need to without being rushed?*

Many working people yearn for the day when they can retire, but overlook the possibility of making their present lives look a little more like retirement right now. What is the desired activity that retirement promises to make possible? More time for hobbies, getting together with friends and family, or just taking it easy? To be able to enjoy these without waiting, we might ask: *What less satisfying volunteer commitments or meetings in our non-job lives could be gradually eliminated to make more time now? Could housekeeping chores be simplified without sacrificing cleanliness and order? Could the time we spend watching television or talking on the phone be cut back? Could neighbors form co-ops for child care or meal preparation? Would it be possible to work more hours for a few days and then take a whole day off?* Disencumbering oneself of organizational duties and externally derived expectations can be marvelously freeing.

Thirdly, simple living means paying attention to our ordinary lives moment by moment, *being present in the here and now*. Fortunately for our happiness, it is not really possible to live in the past or the future, but we constantly try to do this in our minds. When we think about the past, we mostly dwell on our regrets or disappointments; when we think about the future, we are often caught up in anxiety or fear. Such thinking keeps our attention away from being able to listen, speak and act in ways that bring more clarity to the situation right in front of us.

In Leo Tolstoy's story "Three Questions,"[1] a king seeks answers on how to live effectively. The king's questions are these: When is the right time to do something? Who are the most important people? What is the most important thing to do? The king disguises himself as a peasant and journeys up into the mountains to seek advice from a wise hermit. When he arrives, the disguised king leaves his bodyguards to wait out of sight a little distance below. The hermit, who is digging his garden, doesn't answer the king's questions. Noticing that the hermit is elderly and tired, the king helps with the digging, which delays the king's departure. Then when an injured man suddenly appears on the scene, the king takes care of him, dressing his wounds. The injured man subsequently reveals that he is an old enemy who had sought to kill the king in revenge for the man's brother's death at the king's hands. However, while waiting below to ambush and kill the king, the man had been wounded by the king's bodyguards. Now that the king has saved his life, the man begs forgiveness and offers his faithful service.

Before the king leaves, he again asks his three questions of the hermit, who replies that the questions have already been answered. Helping the hermit dig when he needed help delayed the king's departure. That additional interval of time meant his enemy's intention to attack the king was thwarted by the royal bodyguards; thus, the right time is now. "Now! It is the most important time because it is the only time when we have any power," writes Tolstoy. Dressing the injured enemy's wounds turned that enemy into a friend. Thus, the most important person is the one we're with, and the most important action is to do good to that person.

Had the king been preoccupied with his need to get the questions answered when he first arrived at the hermit's hut, and left in impatience when the hermit didn't answer him, the king would have been murdered by his enemy. Had the king not been compassionate to the injured man, the man would probably have died and his heirs would have continued to seek revenge on the king. By doing what he did, the king learned the answers to his questions through life experience, rather than getting someone's opinion.

Although our choices may not involve life-and-death situations like those of the king in this story, we may miss great opportunities if we do not keep our attention in the present, and try to do good right where we find ourselves instead of being lost in the past or the future. Questions we can ask about our focus are these: *Am I present in my life most of the time, or am I often fantasizing about the future, daydreaming or going over past events? Do I pay enough attention to be open to helping the person with me right now?*

Daniel Goleman, psychologist and author of the bestselling *Emotional Intelligence* and *Social Intelligence*, speaks of paying attention as a way to be more fully compassionate: "The first step in compassion is to notice the other's need . . . the enemy of compassion is preoccupation with the self."[2] Noticing others' needs has for most of us become less likely to happen, because we have become increasingly distracted by busyness, ubiquitous entertainment and other material pursuits. Efforts to focus our attention through meditation have been criticized by some people as too self-indulgent, benefiting no one except possibly the meditator. From the standpoint of recent discoveries in neuroscience, however, Goleman offers a practical answer to this objection. Our meditative calmness can actually help others, he says, "not just in some metaphorical way, but actually, in hard scientific terms. . . . If you have a loved one who is suffering, and you yourself are calm, equanimous and loving, your presence is going to help them. It's more than just a nice thing to do; it's an effective thing to do."

We also need to notice when our attention goes outward in wanting something we perceive as exciting or pleasurable; and when our attention turns inward in aversion to something we perceive as threatening or painful. These responses destroy peace and prevent us from experiencing the present moment calmly and fully.

We can learn to be more alert when we find ourselves daydreaming or worrying, desiring or rejecting, so as not to be carried away by these thoughts. They're just thoughts passing through, and we need to let them pass through rather than reaching out, grasping and exploring them, arranging them in sequence, feeding on them, trying to make desired results happen, and warding off undesired ones. This is not to say that we never plan for the future or review and learn from what happened in the past, but that we are wise to limit the time we spend inside our heads, somewhere other than in the present moment.

Dogen, a famous thirteenth-century Japanese Zen master, wrote:

> Above all, don't wish to become a future Buddha;
> Your only concern should be,
> As thought follows thought,
> To avoid clinging to any of them.

If we can reduce our consumption, pare down our schedules and pay attention to the present moment, we can enjoy greater peace ourselves, and make greater peace possible for people, other living creatures and the planet.

Personal Obstacles to Peace

Chapter One

Careless Eating and Drinking

When we think of ways to practice peace, we may not think about our dietary habits, yet they have a huge influence. In this chapter we'll consider the humane, environmental and health reasons that make vegetarian living the most peace-promoting lifestyle, the benefits of eating "real" food instead of processed substitutes, the importance of exercise, and some thoughts about the drinking of alcohol.

What we choose to eat is critically important, because it determines how much violence we do to other creatures and the earth in order to obtain our food. If we want to keep that violence to a minimum, we will choose to eat only organically grown plant foods. The most violent diet, as we will see, is one that includes meat, poultry, eggs, fish and dairy products. Animal suffering is only one aspect of meat eating; we also must consider the serious environmental damage caused by livestock agriculture, as well as its gross inefficiency in feeding people. Furthermore, excessive consumption of meat and dairy products seriously undermines our health. Because the practice of meat eating still enjoys strong societal approval, even while causing suffering to animals, people and the planet, we need to explore these issues thoroughly.

The most convincing reason why practical peacemakers would want to avoid eating meat is direct and basic: it requires monstrous violence to feed a society a meat-centered diet. The number of land animals slaughtered every year in the U.S. is currently *10.1 billion*,[1] and that doesn't count fish and other sea animals, or land animals who died on the farm or in transit to the slaughterhouse. Over ten billion per year translates to a kill rate of approximately *320 per second*, every day, seven days a week. These animals want to live, just as you and I do, and the so-called "humane slaughter" methods—an oxymoron if ever there was one—do not always work as intended. In what may be up to ten percent of the time, especially in the case of chickens, animals are not successfully stunned and are still conscious when bled to death. By not requiring the killing of even one of these animals, *going vegetarian makes the most powerful statement for peace we can possibly make.*

Some readers may think that taking plants for food is also violent because plants have been shown to have some sensitivity. However, unlike animals, plants do not have a central nervous system, and cannot run away when threatened, so it's highly unlikely that pulling a carrot from the ground causes the same amount of pain as killing a chicken. But even someone who believes the suffering is equal would still want to eat plants instead of animals. This is because far more plant lives are saved if plants are eaten directly by people than if plants are first fed to animals and then a person eats that animal's flesh. And, unlike meat, most plant foods we eat do not require the taking of the host creature's life in order to obtain the food. The trees and plants providing our fruits, nuts, legumes, grains, and most vegetables survive our taking the part we eat. Only in the case of root vegetables such as carrots and onions must we kill the whole plant to get the food part.

The question to ask is: *Do my food choices require the confinement and slaughter of other animals?* We cannot be perfectly harmless, of course; not even the most committed vegan can avoid taking some life. Even in farming organically, some insects are killed and unwanted plants—we call them weeds—removed in order to grow our food crops. But by choosing plant foods to eat, we at least greatly minimize the suffering caused to feed us.

What about the use of our precious natural resources? If we want world peace, our environmental resources such as air, water, topsoil, forests and grasslands need to be used with respect, shared with all beings, and preserved to the very best of our ability for the future. Of all human activities that impact the earth, including logging, mining, and the building of highways and shopping centers, the one with the greatest detrimental effect on the earth is agriculture, both farming and livestock agriculture. Agriculture is an essential task in order to feed everyone, so we obviously can't dispense with it, and the number of human mouths to feed keeps increasing while our farmable land area does not. Therefore we need to become as efficient as possible in order to feed the maximum number of people. Efficiency is also needed to preserve wildlife habitat, such as forests and grasslands, which keeps our air clean and supports biodiversity.

Turning our attention to efficient food production leads us to ask what we can grow that will feed the greatest number of people per unit of agricultural land, and the answer to that question leads us clearly to plant foods rather than livestock. When we look at the food crops we're growing now, we find that we feed far more crops to animals than to people. According to the National Corn Growers Association, about *eighty percent* of all corn grown in the U.S. is consumed by domestic and overseas livestock, poultry, and fish production. The United Soybean Board reports the same percent of U.S. soybean production also going to feed livestock.[2]

If we received the same caloric value from eating the meat of these animals as we would receive from eating the plant foods directly, a case for livestock might still be made. However, there is a huge loss of food value; even in the best circumstances we lose about two-thirds of the calories of the plant foods if we send them through animals and then eat those animals' flesh. Losses are usually even greater, ranging to nine-tenths of available plant calories or more. If we had a piece of farmland the size of a football field, we could feed only two people if we raised cattle on it, but up to sixty people if we planted it in soybeans.

If we stopped breeding and feeding cattle, pigs and chickens on these crops, and ate these plant foods directly, we'd only need to farm one-seventh to one-tenth of the land we currently farm. This would enable us to remove from production the marginal land, areas that require irrigation or other inputs to be arable, and let much more acreage remain as forests or wetlands. Farming so much less land would preserve topsoil, which erodes when land is plowed, as well as reduce our use of fossil fuel-derived fertilizers and pesticides. Another savings of energy is that needed for the refrigeration of meat, cheese or eggs, much greater than what is needed for legumes or grains.

The second reason to use our farmland for crops to be fed directly to people, rather than to raise livestock, is for better health. None of this bloodshed of animal slaughter or inefficiency of livestock agriculture is necessary or even desirable for our health, because we can enjoy better health without animal products. In the Global South, illnesses that kill include dysentery, cholera, typhoid, tuberculosis, complications from childbirth, and malnutrition. Having mostly eradicated these in the West, one might think we'd be quite healthy. But instead, we've replaced diseases of unsanitary conditions and poverty with diseases of affluence, of rich diets and sedentary habits. The diseases that consume the lion's share of all health care costs—and the major killers of Americans—are heart disease, stroke, cancer, and diabetes. The diseases of affluence arise from a diet high in meat and dairy products, rich pastries and fried foods; these are high in animal fat and protein while low in fiber, the "good" carbohydrates, and antioxidants. There is a simple, effective, no-side-effects, noninvasive response to the diseases of affluence that would keep health care costs low. We need to show people how, and give them social support, to change their diets to low-fat unrefined plant foods. Drs. John McDougall, Neal Barnard, and others have been doing exactly this for decades, and it works.

We know that obesity is a risk factor for a number of dangerous diseases. Eating diets high in animal products makes us more likely to be overweight, because such calorie-dense foods give us more calories than we can handle without filling us up. This lack of satisfaction leads us to keep eating beyond the point at which we should stop. For example, imagine eating 500 calories of rice and beans, and then imagine eating, at another time, 500 calories of cheese. The rice and beans would occupy a much greater volume in your stomach, so you would begin to feel full without eating so many calories that you would gain weight. With the 500 calories of cheese, however, your stomach would not be full, thus causing you to still feel hungry, and you would keep eating.

High rates of preventable disease are costly, putting considerable financial pressure on individuals and governments, and making health care increasingly expensive. Such diseases disrupt the harmony of families, adding stress that can readily destroy their peace, and drive up the cost of health insurance, so that millions of people must go without it.

Another health-oriented reason to avoid animal products is that deadly strains of influenza begin as diseases of livestock, such as swine flu and avian flu, and then mutate to infect humans. Epidemics of these diseases have definitely robbed us of our peace, creating medical emergency situations and killing millions of people. There are also the infectious neurological diseases that jump from livestock to humans, such as variant CJD, commonly known as mad cow disease. If we did not keep livestock, these dangerous diseases would be nearly eliminated.

Eating "lower on the food chain" is often advised for more intentional living, but what this means isn't always spelled out. The question to ask when we're deciding what food to buy, either at the supermarket or restaurant, is: *Does this food come from a plant or an animal?* For example, we are buying a taco or burrito in a restaurant. We can choose one with either beef or beans, so it's easy to choose beans. We can explore ethnic cuisines—Chinese, Thai, Mexican, Middle Eastern, Indian, and most others—in which plant foods are abundant. We can eat in vegetarian restaurants, adapt familiar dishes like spaghetti, chili, or pizza to vegetarian versions. Compared to what was available even a few years ago, we now have dozens of easy and delicious vegetarian recipes available in cookbooks and online, and we can buy veggie convenience foods in many supermarkets. Of all the changes we can make in living more simply, going vegetarian does the most and gives us the personal benefit of better health.

We can create support for vegetarian living in our spiritual communities, encouraging the preparation of vegetarian food for group dinners and the sharing of vegetarian recipes. Readers whose spiritual leaders are not vegetarians can bring to their attention the issues considered in this chapter. Christian readers who encounter the excuse that Jesus ate meat will want to familiarize themselves with the historical evidence to the contrary.[3]

Simple living includes not only a vegetarian diet but also the habit of eating real food instead of processed food components laced with unpronounceable chemicals. As people simplify their needs and thus need to work fewer hours, they will be able to stay home more. As a result, families and communities will become stronger, leading to more interaction and a greater likelihood of sharing meals instead of grabbing them on the run or eating alone. Sharing a meal usually means eating more slowly, which allows our stomach's signal that it is full to reach our minds before we have stuffed ourselves. People will have the time and inclination to cook real food, which is bound to be more healthful, instead of driving to a fast food restaurant or heating up a microwaveable entrée.

As we come to eat food that tastes really good, we'll come to appreciate it more. More of us might try growing some of our own, but in any case, we'll be less likely to take it for granted and overindulge. Food becomes a way we connect with all life on earth, not just fuel to keep ourselves going.

As we learn to replace some of our driving with walking or biking, another practice of simple living, we'll get more exercise. Doctors tell us that even a few minutes of walking every day can make a huge difference. According to the Trust for America's Health, the U.S. would save $5.6 *billion* annually in costs associated with treating heart disease if just *one-tenth* of Americans began walking regularly.[4] As a bonus, those who walk may get to know their neighbors better, which will strengthen the feeling of community and reduce the stress of isolation. In his book *Love and Survival*, Dr. Dean Ornish cites studies that show the profound impact on our health of having positive relationships with friends and family members. Giving and receiving love translates as stronger immune systems, better cardiovascular functioning and longer life expectancies.[5]

In addition, more exercise will put us more in tune with our bodies, and we may come to respect them for the marvelous organisms they are. More respect will lead in turn to more mindful eating and drinking, which, hand in hand with the exercise, will improve our health and wellbeing.

The drinking of alcohol to excess leads to extensive damage to health, destroys social and familial peace, and takes thousands of lives every year in traffic accidents. How do we, who aspire to be practical peacemakers, approach the issue of drinking? Thich Nhat Hanh teaches a sensible reason for abstinence. He points out that individually we may be able to drink responsibly, never getting drunk or out of control, but we need to consider the example we set. Even by having only one or two drinks, we convey acceptance of alcohol in our homes and in our lives, and we are supporting those who produce alcoholic beverages. (Buddhist readers may know that dealing in intoxicants and raising animals for slaughter are two of the five livelihoods the Buddha urged followers to avoid. The other three are dealing in deadly weapons, slavery, and poisons.) The acceptance and support we give to the drinking of alcohol may not cause us any problems personally, but how do we know what others who see us drink will do? They will be more likely to drink, following our example, but, unlike the responsible drinker, they may be potential alcoholics. Our encouragement may get them started on the path to addiction and the suffering that follows. If by not serving alcohol in our homes, and by abstaining when we socialize with others, we can prevent even a small portion of the disease, domestic violence, and drunk-driving deaths that arise from alcohol abuse, isn't it worthwhile to do so?

Thich Nhat Hanh also points out the huge amounts of grain necessary to produce alcohol and meat, grain desperately needed to feed hungry people. "Alcohol is directly related to the suffering of children. For instance, to make one glass of rice wine takes a whole basket of rice. Every day 40,000 children die in the world for lack of food. We who overeat in the West, who are feeding grains to animals to make meat, are eating the flesh of these children."[6]

There is abundant information on healthful living for those who want to remove their support of slaughterhouse violence, abstain from alcoholic beverages, decrease their risk of disease, enjoy good health, and eat in the way that feeds the most people using the least land to do so. What are you waiting for?

Chapter Two

Overcommitting Our Time

One of the most common effects of our overconsumptive lives is time pressure, the stress caused by planning more activities for a given time period than can be reasonably achieved. Time pressure shatters our ability to act peacefully. Why has simplifying in this area been such a difficult lesson for many people? Because we want to expand the number of experiences we and our families can enjoy, assuming without question that to do so will make us happier, and/or our children smarter. But does it?

Americans' average workweek is longer than it was a few decades ago. For some it is necessary to work more hours, perhaps even two jobs, just to make ends meet, as real income declines. The general trend in society, however, has been to work longer hours to be able to afford more consumer goods, instead of being willing to forego some toys and larger houses in order to have more spare time. As it is, adults and kids have activities scheduled for every moment from awakening to bedtime, again assuming without question that unplanned time is wasted time. I'm not sure how this erroneous belief originated, but rather than enhancing life, it has done untold harm to our physical and mental wellbeing, while destroying our personal peacefulness. It has often caused us to treat others curtly, or even rudely. I knew when I noticed myself leaving one gathering of friends early, only to arrive late to another gathering, that I needed to take a serious look at how I was planning my time. This issue of time stress is the traditional territory of many books on simple living; we'll briefly summarize it here.

Living more simply can reduce time pressure by shortening our commute to work, as we reorganize our lives to live closer to our work or work from home. Less driving means less peace-destroying stress. If we can bike or walk, we can combine our commute with the time we'd otherwise set aside for some type of physical exercise, giving us more free time.

Once we stop buying so much stuff, we will reduce the time needed for shopping. I can recall that many years ago I wanted to wear the latest fashions, including shoes and handbags that match. After we simplify, our former complaint of "I have absolutely nothing to wear" becomes "I have so much I never wear—why am I buying so much?" When we simplify our wardrobes, we come to see that fashion is just another way to get us to spend our life energy on inconsequential things. We may still splurge on a fashion item occasionally, but knowing something of the environmental impact of the garment means we will consider the purchase carefully. Even a T-shirt has a pesticide impact in growing the cotton, a fossil fuel impact in making the polyester, a fair labor issue if it was made in a sweatshop, and the CO_2 impact of shipping it around the world from China. We can much more readily justify a purchase if we buy it used. Becoming more conscious about our wardrobe doesn't mean we won't be neat in appearance, but that we'll gravitate to classic styles that look good regardless of what's "in" at the moment. And we may even develop our own style that will suit us better than the latest fashions.

I also wanted to own the latest music recordings, to buy kitchen gadgets and gourmet foods, expensive vacations, and so on. All that wanting takes time—and money—to satisfy. Now I enjoy replaying favorite recordings and borrowing newer ones from the library. Acquiring music and other content through downloads may save some time and money, and it definitely reduces our accumulation of stuff to store. I discovered that the extra kitchen gadgets just cluttered my shelves and drawers, and that the important part of a vacation is just taking time out for a change of scene. Getaways can be nearby as well as faraway, and when we realize the climatic impact of burning fossil fuels for pleasure trips, especially when we travel by air, we find nearby getaways much more satisfying to take.

What a joy it is when we can say "no" to commitments that don't enrich us! We need to forget what we feel we "ought" to do and concentrate on activities—or lack of them—that will permit us a saner life. The things we really ought to do, much fewer in number than we'd perhaps thought, will gradually become apparent, and we can add them back in. In time—and it does take some time to slow down enough—we may be able to leave half-days, or even full days, entirely unplanned.

As we learn not to overschedule ourselves, we'll help our kids do the same, which will make them happier, while freeing parents from so much time-consuming chauffeuring. If the kids can walk to school, not only can parents save driving, but the kids also get a fitness benefit and a better acquaintance with their neighbors.

Simplifying usually brings with it the benefit of reducing our expenses. If we can simplify enough for one adult to quit work and be a stay-at-home parent, the cooking, cleaning and other homemaking tasks can be managed with much less stress. One of the classic descriptions of how a motivated mother became frugal enough to stay at home, even though her husband's salary was only average, is that of Amy Dacyczyn, whose cheerful and practical *Tightwad Gazette* newsletters were collected into books to inspire others.[1]

Our lives become so satisfying that we don't need to escape so much, so we reduce the time we spend attending entertainment events. We get so that our everyday tasks, like caring for family and companion animals, cooking wholesome food from scratch, gardening, building needed items, and talking with friends, provide much of our entertainment. We have enough time to exercise, which in itself promotes stress reduction, as does connecting more with friends and family. We'll still want to see a new movie, play or other event occasionally, but it won't be a sort of frantic effort to keep up with everything new.

Once we have freed our lives of meaningless activities, we learn to allow more time for each task than we think it will take, so that if something unexpected does come up, we can still be calm and unruffled, and get everything necessary done. Once we start leaving breathing space between appointments, instead of scheduling them back to back, we can bring along reading material or knitting to fill any time between appointments, or perhaps sit quietly and people-watch, or, if the weather cooperates, take a short walk. We may find ourselves with just enough extra time in our lives to visit an older person, or undertake a charity project or other worthwhile activity.

Ultimately, when we allow enough time for everything, we can always give our close attention where it is needed, rather than rushing through life wondering why we feel unfulfilled.

Chapter Three

Instant Gratification

Many of the daily decisions we make pit short-term and long-term rewards against each other. Shall I enjoy the sweet taste of a couple of doughnuts now, or shall I enjoy the pleasure of maintaining a trim weight? Shall I enjoy the luxury of skipping my morning walk in favor of lounging around reading the newspaper, or shall I discipline myself to exercise in order to enjoy better health in the long term? Shall I choose the momentary high of a new luxury purchase, or the long-term reward of saving that money and being more financially secure in the future? Shall I give in to the momentary ego satisfaction of venting anger and blame, or shall I pause and consider before making a response I may regret? A practical peacemaker adopts a healthy skepticism toward instant gratification, having learned that the long-term rewards are usually the ones that lead to peace. "If there is a conflict between the short-term interest and the long-term interest, the long-term interest is more important," writes the Dalai

Lama.[1] Let's look at the previous examples more closely.

Foregoing extra sweets and snacks in order to maintain our health and a trim weight means we will feel better and thus be more able to contribute as citizens. This is not meant to imply that overweight people do not contribute, far from it; however, the better we feel, the more energy we have. In refusing surplus empty calories, we avoid causing the stress to ourselves and our loved ones that we would cause if we gained excessive weight and succumbed to chronic illness before our time. We also will not be contributing to the sharp rise in health care costs that threatens national economic stability. We will be supporting with our purchases the food vendors whose products promote health, rather than those whose products lead to obesity and ill health. This is not to say we can never have junk food, just that it needs to be the exception rather than the rule. The more unhealthful indulgences we allow ourselves, the more we establish such indulgence as a habit.

Ah, exercise—a challenging area of self-discipline for many of us! How seductive it can seem, "just this once," to skip our workout to relax. We can so easily convince ourselves how hard we've been working this week and how we deserve to take a break. This kind of self-talk is at its most persuasive when we are not fully awake and able to evaluate the decision coherently. We fall back asleep quickly and effortlessly, and the window of time available for exercise is lost. Later in the day, when we are alert and clearheaded, we can see that we sabotaged our fitness goals—again!—which may cause feelings of guilt and failure, certainly not a peaceful state. We note our sluggishness, the absence of that wonderful humming physical high that comes after exercise. We may carry irritability into the rest of our day, affecting our ability to be peaceful in our interactions with others. As in the previous example, this is not to say we can never skip a workout if there is a good reason to do so, just to advise that it should not become habitual.

Spending money on something exciting will nearly always have a greater immediate appeal than saving that money, yet when tempted we need to stay present in the here and now and evaluate the situation carefully. Certainly the environment will benefit if we decide to purchase fewer unneeded goods, a definitely peaceful result. The thrill of luxury purchases diminishes if we buy to excess; excitement turns to boredom. Saving money falls out of fashion when credit is easy to obtain.

I recall a family story about my grandmother's older sister. At the turn of the twentieth century, when she was young and in love, her sweetheart proposed. Before they got married, however, he wanted them to have enough money saved to buy a house. Women who were teachers, as she was, were required to quit their jobs if they got married, so remaining single was the only way she could keep earning money.

Staying single was also the best strategy for him, as it meant he had only himself to support, rather than the additional expenses of a wife and any children who might come along. The years passed and they continued working and saving. Ultimately, it took them *ten years* to save enough. Finally, in 1910, when he was thirty-two and she twenty-nine, they married, moved into their own home, and remained married to the end of their lives. When this story about their courtship was told at family gatherings, there was some amusement at the young man's pride and stubbornness, but underneath it was admiration that he was sufficiently disciplined to save enough to purchase a home, and to remain committed to his fiancée through a ten-year engagement. Now, of course, a woman can easily earn money while married, and readily available contraceptive options can prevent any surprise pregnancies. Still, couples have difficulty saving money.

When people are given the hypothetical choice of spending five dollars a week on lottery tickets or saving that money, and are asked which is more likely to result in a long-term financial benefit, the majority say the lottery tickets. They fail to realize either the odds of winning the lottery, or how much five dollars a week will amount to, with compound interest, in twenty or thirty years.

Consider this example of the power of compound interest. If Christopher Columbus had placed a single penny in a six percent interest-bearing account in 1492 and instructed someone to remove the interest every year, the value of the interest earned by 2007 would be 31 cents. But if he had placed the same penny into the same interest-bearing account but left the earned interest to compound—earning interest upon the interest—the resulting balance for 515 years would be over $95 billion![2] Even though we don't have 515 years to accumulate a nest egg, it is astounding how compound interest makes our money grow.

Our inability to save has reached alarming proportions. We're not talking about a low rate of savings, or no savings; we're talking about having to borrow to make ends meet. For the first time since the Great Depression, according to the U.S. Department of Commerce, the savings rate for 2006 was *negative one percent*.[3] This means that Americans on average spent all that they earned and also either borrowed or spent part of their savings! We've come as far as we possibly can from the "a penny saved is a penny earned" advice of our elders. We display either an astonishing lack of discipline in our personal finances, or perhaps a foolish overconfidence that there will be no "rainy days" of job loss or illness to face in the near future. A news story commented, "Consumers depleted their savings to finance the purchase of cars and other big-ticket items."[4] In a later chapter we'll see the role that advertising plays in leading us down this primrose path. Living without a safety net is risky behavior indeed.

Choosing instant gratification in sexual relationships can

cause a great deal of suffering, including profound emotional turmoil, deeply felt betrayal and guilt, divorce, alienated children, sexually transmitted diseases and unwanted pregnancies. Popular media tend to minimize or ignore these consequences, sometimes even glamorizing irresponsible sexual behavior. In the enchantment of attraction and the heat of passion, one may not even think of what harm may be caused by the failure to regard the new partner as a person with emotional needs for love, care and trustworthiness. One may be momentarily oblivious to commitments made to spouses or other longtime partners, the violation of which can be gut-wrenchingly painful and even lead to violence, as countless love triangle murders and suicides attest. Even if no actual violence results, we find many people damaged, operating from the "once bitten, twice shy" mindset, afraid to trust again and thus denying themselves and a potential partner a fulfilling relationship. Such self-imposed isolation and the fear of opening one's heart can have implications for the larger society as well. In addition, millions of children are deeply hurt, grieving, and uprooted, shuttled between divorced parents.

Couples would be well advised to take plenty of time to get to know one another and, if there is no long-term potential, to avoid deepening the relationship beyond friendship. Once in a committed relationship, they need to do their utmost to keep the commitment, except in cases where more harm is done by keeping it than by ending it. Thinking carefully before becoming sexually involved is a giant step toward peace within oneself, in society, and for future generations.

Another area of our experience in which instant gratification is extremely persuasive is anger. An angry response to someone whose action we perceive as unkind can be extremely satisfying in the moment ("I guess I told her! She'll think twice before she does that to me again!"). A more compassionate handling of the situation might have turned an enemy into a friend, an opportunity that is likely to be lost if anger is thoughtlessly vented. The other person may have wanted to be unkind, but it's possible that the action was misinterpreted and no offense was intended. The quick, angry response allows no time to extend the benefit of the doubt, to consider the other person's possible motive, to evaluate other possible responses or to allow compassion to arise for the other person's suffering. Sometimes just returning kindness for perceived unkindness can turn the situation around.

Certainly there are situations where there is no long-term benefit to denying oneself an immediate pleasure. For example, should you eat a bowl of fresh berries offered when you are hungry? Unless you have someone nearby who is not getting enough to eat, your choice is clear—you can go with the obvious short-term benefit—yum! The benefit of not eating them is nonexistent, as your hunger will increase and the fruit will spoil—or someone else will overeat. Should you give a close family member a hug? The short-term pleasure and support is obvious to both, and no long-term benefit accrues in withholding it. You may not see this person again, but in the much more likely case that you will see them, you can give them another hug then. If you need a new dress, you can buy a gorgeous, brightly colored one just as easily as a drab, unflattering one.

The practice of being wary about instant gratification should not be considered dull or joyless or overly methodical. This is no exhortation to being a puritan, defined as one who regards pleasure or luxury as sinful; on the contrary, there is plenty of room for beauty, enjoyment, spontaneity, and occasional luxury. It's just something to ponder as you face each day's choices: Is the alternative with the long-term benefit the one most likely to produce peace?

Chapter Four

Unexamined Opinions

Another potential enemy of peace that is internal rather than external is our habit of holding to unexamined opinions. In the process of everyday living, we come to solidify certain viewpoints on a great variety of people and situations that, over time, seem to us to be the absolute truth. Some of these beliefs serve us well and need no further examination, such as our conviction that stepping out in front of an oncoming truck, or eating poisoned food, would be likely to cause us considerable pain or death. Beliefs of this kind are not limiting or parochial, and in any case are necessary because we cannot conveniently approach every situation as brand-new every time it arises. However, we would be wise to continually observe and modify many of our "fossilized" views that make us certain we know the best way to respond in a given situation.

Let me give a mundane example. We know the way from our home to our work. Back when we first took the job, or first moved into our present home, we considered all the likely ways to get from home to work and chose the one that was shortest or that we liked best. Years have passed and we always go the same way, but one day, due to road construction or some other obstacle, we take a different route. Something has changed; perhaps a natural foods store has opened on the new route and now, if we go this way, we can do our grocery shopping on the way home from work. Due to being forced to take another route, we discover that it is preferable. We change our longstanding habit and go the new way instead.

We may have dogmatic concepts about ourselves, limiting beliefs based on something a parent or teacher said many years ago, or some early failed attempt in a particular activity. Perhaps it related to our intelligence or abilities to master certain kinds of tasks. Let's say we formed the belief that we are not good at public speaking, and perhaps at the time it was an accurate assessment of our ability. Now, however, we have additional years of life experience resulting in greatly increased self-esteem and poise. An ethical or political issue comes to our attention that we feel moved to speak out about. If we cling to the old limiting belief, we won't act. However, if we re-examine the belief and see that it is no longer true, that we are considerably more confident now, and if we spend a little effort working on our understanding of the issue and our delivery technique, we may do quite well speaking at a public meeting. What we say may influence and inspire others, and we will have succeeded in two ways: in overcoming a false belief that constricted our life, and in increasing awareness about some kind of injustice that needs to be exposed. Getting over the fear of public speaking is extremely worthwhile for an aspiring practical peacemaker.

We may have fossilized concepts about others, either individuals we have known or groups we have read about or encountered briefly. In the case of individuals, we may be basing our beliefs on events of years ago, or on an isolated instance of the person's behavior which we chose to interpret in a way that may be far different than what the person intended. In the case of groups, we could have read a biased report in the media, or based our beliefs for the whole group on the irresponsible behavior of one or a few members of that group. We may have accepted unexamined the prejudices of our parents or others who represent authority. We may have formed false judgments about individuals or groups by accepting as true what we hear about them from third parties, through gossip. The words "always" or "never," when applied to beliefs about people or groups, can alert us that here is a dogma that needs to be given some play on the leash. We should also be suspicious if we find ourselves acting in conditioned ways that diminish another's humanity and individuality.

Such unquestioned concepts, no matter how they came to

be formed, can be the seeds of discrimination and rejection, and thus of violence. By carefully considering such beliefs within ourselves, we can learn to act in more open and peaceful ways. By keeping that spaciousness as we encounter our world every day, we can see and respond helpfully to people and to situations we might otherwise not even notice. Consider the opening lines of *Verses on the Faith Mind*, by Zen patriarch Seng-tsan:

> The great Way is not difficult for those who have no preferences.
>
> When love and hatred are both absent, everything becomes clear and undisguised.
>
> Make the smallest distinction, however, and heaven and earth are set infinitely apart.
>
> If you wish to see the truth, then hold no opinions for or against anything.[1]

"Holding no opinions" does not exempt us from ethical behavior. It does not mean we can do whatever we please regardless of the consequences. We must still strive to act with wisdom and compassion, and to uphold the precepts or commandments of our faith tradition. If we are sincere about peace, however, we will not apply them with blind absolutism, advocate punishment or vengeance, or sit in judgment of what we consider our own failures or those of others.

Byron Katie, originator of a technique of self-examination she calls "The Work," invites people to question the painful beliefs they hold.[2] One of the exercises in her weekend seminars invites participants to bring to mind the worst mistake they think they have ever made. The exercise leads them to explore whether they can truly know that it was a mistake, whether they could have known what was best for their path at that time, and whether any good ultimately came of that action. In most cases, the participant realizes that the very action that seemed so terrible was often a turning point toward a better life. We can only come to the understanding we have today by having gone through our so-called mistakes. Through this exercise we not only begin to release the shame and guilt we've been carrying, but may actually come to feel grateful that the painful situation happened as it did.

Once again, being able to keep our attention in the present moment can prevent us from blindly acting in accordance with a belief system we formed in the past. Instead, we will have the presence of mind to evaluate whether the old system is reliable as a basis for ethical behavior, and specifically whether it applies to the situation we face now. Such flexibility will not only prevent some unwise responses on our part, but may also allow us to heal some painful events in our past.

Chapter Five

Anger

Anger is pervasive in modern life, in sharp words spoken or outright domestic violence toward spouses and children, "backstabbing" on the job, criticism of others' motives and actions, malicious gossip, silent seething, road rage and vandalism, to name just a few manifestations. Another more subtle kind of anger arises from the hyperindividualism of our society: the belief that I'm entitled to do what I want whenever I want, use resources as wastefully as I want—and anyone who stands in the way of my instant gratification is my enemy. Our work as practical peacemakers requires us to defuse anger in ourselves and avoid stimulating it in others.

That anger is the enemy of peace is no surprise, although I doubt most people, even people who sincerely desire peace, give it much thought. When anger arises in the mind, a person often loses control and says or does things s/he later may deeply regret. The expression of anger may result in actual physical violence that can kill or injure its object, or it may be confined to words. However, words spoken in the heat of anger, words that belittle, insult or blame, are chosen to inflict as much emotional pain as possible. Such words may fester for many years, seriously undermining self-esteem and stunting the victim's emotional growth. Especially damaging are words directed at children or others who are vulnerable.

My father was one who, although a loving parent and idealistic spiritual seeker, could not control his rage. When frustration mounted, he would suddenly turn on my brother or me with a ferocity that was devastating. He never physically abused either of us, unless spanking is considered to be abuse, and never insulted us, but those angry outbursts nonetheless shattered my ability to feel lovable. I became afraid of him and, by extension, all men, throughout my childhood. Fortunately, as an adult and after he had died, I came to realize that he was more a victim of this anger than I was. I also came to understand some of the factors that led to this behavior, such as difficulties at work, concern about money, and chronic physical pain.

Are there no circumstances, readers may ask, that justify the expression of anger? What about injustice of all kinds, lying and deception by those in power, the betrayal of trust in a friendship or intimate relationship? Surely it is not advisable to hold in or suppress our so-called "righteous" anger; doesn't that lead to high blood pressure, heart attacks and other serious health consequences? Doesn't it make us likely to blow up later at a person or animal who is innocent?

There is an important middle ground between expressing angry behavior and holding it all in: we can repeatedly and determinedly call attention to an unjust situation and seek its redress, but without losing emotional control. This was expertly modeled for us by Jesus' expelling from the Temple those who were selling animals to be sacrificed, by Gandhi's salt march to the sea, by Kent State students putting flowers in the barrels of guns held by National Guard troops, by everyone who has responded to violence nonviolently. Is it always successful? Yes and no. It may not always be successful according to the world's judgment of success. In the examples above, Jesus lost his life as a result of his action, as did four of the Kent State students; Gandhi's faction won independence but was unable to stop sectarian violence between Hindus and Muslims. Yet, in at least two ways, nonviolent action is *always* successful: it allows the one who is outraged a powerful way to bear witness and make the injustice known to the world, which will likely inspire others; and it does not intensify or escalate the injustice, as a vindictive or violent response would do.

Although *expression* of anger inflicts suffering on others, *suppression* of anger, turning it inward to inflict suffering on oneself, is not the answer either. What we want to work toward is *transformation* of the anger, that is, noticing when it arises in us and learning constructive ways to deal with it. It takes a great deal of mental alertness and presence to stop the force of our fury. Without the ability to pause and notice what is happening in us, the anger just takes over and out come the hurtful words or deeds. Some kind of daily meditative practice is needed to teach us to observe our thoughts and be able to act on them or not, so step one is just that: *a regular daily practice of silently noticing our thoughts or following our breath* so as to slow down and separate our thoughts, one from another. Even a few minutes a day can be helpful: count each breath, in and out, up to ten, and then start over. When the mind darts off in this or that direction, which it undoubtedly will, we just gently bring it back to the counting. Through this kind of practice, we develop awareness of what we are thinking at any given moment, and can learn to ride the horse of our mind instead of allowing the horse to bolt and drag us painfully through the mud of explosive anger. We become aware of our own impulses toward greed and selfishness, and learn to pause and perhaps make another choice.

A second prerequisite for this work is what we could call "Compassion 101," *the development of a basic empathy with those who express anger.* Surely no one who is angry is happy or fulfilled, and anger is known to cause stress to the body. Angry people may think they get some satisfaction from expressing their anger, but it usually backfires to further frustrate their life. Once we understand that angry people are suffering, compassion for them—and detachment from their outbursts—comes more easily. We do not need to know the nature of their suffering, but need only to reflect on how unhappy they must be in order to act in such harmful ways.

We can deepen our grasp of everyday compassion by reflecting not only on how unhappy other angry persons must be, but by turning our attention to the times when we ourselves have been angry. How did it feel, physically and emotionally, to be angry? Was it enjoyable? Were we suffering at the time? Can anger ever truly be a source of pride or power? When angry, have we said or done things we later regretted? It soon becomes clear that we cannot be peacemakers so long as we still routinely express anger, and in this realization our aspiration to control and ultimately transform our anger is greatly strengthened.

Third, we need to *take a hard look at the ways in which we water the seeds of anger in others*. We may poke fun at others, assuming they're "good sports" who can take a little "sparring" in the name of friendship, but can we be certain it's positive and enjoyable for them? If there is any doubt, we need to stop that behavior, and instead seek to point out their positive qualities. Do we ever drive aggressively or act rudely to those who serve us? The anger that our behavior triggers in others may have harmful consequences far beyond what we could possibly foresee, as they pass it on to other people in their lives.

How about criticism of those we live with: spouses,

partners, children, roommates? They are the ones we may treat the worst sometimes, because they are there amidst our everyday frustrations. *We need to learn practical skills to resolve disputes as they arise.* If a difficulty in a family relationship needs to be addressed, it should be done when we are calm, at a time appropriately chosen for everyone involved, when there is enough time to hear everyone out. In speaking of the behavior we wish to change, we must give the maximum benefit of the doubt to the offender, and honestly try to understand the suffering in him or her that gave rise to the action. To accomplish this, we must listen carefully and lovingly, and speak in "I" phrases, for example, "When it's your turn to clean up the dishes but you leave them undone, I am unhappy trying to cook the next meal amid the mess. I then have to do your job, which doesn't seem fair." How much more likely this is to motivate a positive change than to point a finger of blame: "You are a lazy good-for-nothing son to leave the dirty dishes undone."

A further rule of loving speech is to refrain from bringing up any way at all in which this person has disappointed you in the past. People cannot change what they did in the past, and they may in fact be ashamed of their behavior, even if they have never admitted it to you or perhaps even to themselves. Bringing up past behavior reinforces their shame, their resentment of you for holding it over them, and their frustration in not being able to change the past. It is also likely to make them feel powerless to change: "That's just the way I am."

I am no expert on family communications, but I believe these five guidelines can make a world of difference in resolving disputes. To summarize: 1) bring up the matter when you are calm and the other person is in a receptive mood, 2) activate your compassion, assuming that the other person must be suffering to have acted thoughtlessly, 3) make an effort to hear the other person out and understand his or her side of the story, 4) speak in sentences that begin with "I" instead of "you," and 5) leave the other person's past behavior out of the discussion.

Another chance to defuse anger is when our friends want to tell us about a time they were angry, a response they will almost certainly see as justifiable. Instead of tut-tutting in support of how wronged they were, we can gently direct their attention to the fact that the perpetrator of the outrage must be suffering as much as they are, or more. We may also be able to explore with them other, more constructive ways they might have reacted and can react in the future when a similar situation arises.

If we can notice when our own anger arises, refrain from acting on it, and seek systematically to transform it, and if we can avoid behaviors that incite or reinforce anger in others, we will make a considerable practical contribution to peace in our corner of the world.

Societal Obstacles to Peace

Chapter Six

Advertising without Accountability

One of the most powerful forces in our society that keeps us overconsuming, overspending, risking our health, cluttering our homes and our lives with unnecessary possessions, and endangering our planet's future, is advertising. This is a multibillion-dollar industry that panders to our greed and insecurity in ways that it hopes we won't notice.

Commercials and magazine advertisements do their utmost to get us to want a particular product or service, or, even better, to get us to think we *need* it. The more stuff we buy, the ads persuade us, the more attractive, secure, socially or sexually sought out, "cool," or successful we will be. They never mention, of course, that most of these implications are utterly absurd and often outright deceptive. Using a certain brand of shampoo or toothpaste will not make our hair or teeth more beautiful than using another similar brand. If the kind of car we buy attracts a partner to us, we should be hesitant instead of thrilled about the partner, because s/he is evidently more interested in the car than in us. In addition, asking us to connect a glamorous partner—usually a woman—with a purchase objectifies her in an offensive way. It communicates that her worth depends on her beauty, and that her affections can be bought. That brand of soft drink made to look so appealing will decay our teeth, add empty, even harmful calories, and probably cause us to drink less water, which is what our thirst is telling us we need. Repeatedly pitching sodas, chips, doughnuts, and candy contributes to our obesity crisis. Having expensive jewelry or new furniture will not make a troubled marriage better. We could go on and on. Yet even the most careful among us can get caught up in the images and the hype.

Advertising carries another insidious message: whatever you are now is not good enough. This runs the gamut from teaching you that "the toothpaste you're using now was a poor choice" to "spending your money on nonessentials will enrich your life more than saving money would" to "you can't be a good mother unless you buy this magazine and learn how" to "the partner you chose is not making you as happy as a more glamorous one would." The ads are planting and constantly reinforcing in your mind that your decisions are poorly made, your skills are inadequate, you're not really enjoying your life, you don't have enough money, you're socially inept; in short, you're a loser. And furthermore, that the way to greater satisfaction is not to be more grateful for what you have, not to work on areas that need to be improved, not to reach out to help others, and above all not to trust yourself, but to *buy something*.

Another truth the ads fail to mention is that buying a lot of stuff can break one's budget, engendering feelings of guilt or failure, and possibly leading to serious debt. Why are so many people maxed out on credit cards? For some it may be for necessities, especially during a crisis of unemployment or illness, but for most people it is for luxury items, additional clothing, or expensive entertainment, trips, or gifts that advertising stimulated them to buy. The level of personal savings in the U.S., as we noted earlier, is in fact below zero! Even if we successfully avoid the slippery slope into debt, buying unneeded stuff means that we must work more hours to pay for it, hours subtracted from relaxing, spending time with loved ones, improving our education, or enjoying creative pursuits. The stuff must also be stored—which may lead to further financial obligation to rent a storage unit or buy a bigger house—and maintained, which takes more time and money for cleaning and repairs. In some newer neighborhoods, three-car garages seem to be the norm— insanity! Think of the hours someone must work to buy, maintain and insure three cars, in addition to the pollution they cause when driven. Think of the land area taken up by the roads and garage space that would be needed if every family owned three cars. We work more hours to spend more to buy, store, and maintain more stuff that, beyond the level of what we need to be comfortable, does not bring lasting happiness. Wake up, America!

Ads take up ever greater amounts of time in the average hour of television watching. Before 1985, the FCC regulated how much advertising time could be sold per hour of programming, but in that year deregulation occurred, allowing the stations to sell as much time as they think viewers will tolerate. By 2000, the advertising time per hour of prime time programming had crept up to thirteen minutes for adult programs, and even more for children's programs.[1] In recent years there has been a major shift of advertising dollars— to the tune of $40 *billion* annually—to appeal directly to children, teaching them to want, in fact demand, the specific products they see advertised. Too young to see through the deceptive claims of the ads—for example, that owning a certain toy will make them permanently happy and popular with other kids—children become pawns in the hands of the advertisers. Very young children are not able to distinguish the ads from the program, so are especially vulnerable, but can recognize brand logos as young as age two.

In his book *Con$umed*, Benjamin R. Barber makes the case that along with children being heavily targeted, advertisers encourage adults to remain adolescent. Cultivating extended psychological adolescence "nurtures a culture of impetuous consumption necessary to selling puerile goods in a developed world that has few genuine needs."[2]

This is done by glamorizing consumption without regard for consequences, short-term pleasure without long-term responsibility, whatever is easy instead of that which takes time and care to establish. "What is easy may also turn out to be less gratifying, hampering rather than furthering human happiness . . . Under the cultural sway of infantilization this lesson is made to seem rigid and Puritanical, the preserve of people who are hostile to happiness."[3]

Just as advertising time as a percentage of television programming has increased, so has the space ads take up in a big city Sunday newspaper. Retail stores now include a multi-page slick color sales brochure, rather than a one- or two-page ad in the body of the newspaper. This requires more trees to be cut to print these additional pages, more weight for the home delivery person to carry around, more time required for the subscriber to go through the paper, more temptation to buy unneeded merchandise, and much greater weight of newsprint to be recycled or perhaps simply landfilled.

Advertising assaults us everywhere, including areas that used to be free of any product endorsements: the external surfaces of clothing, shoes, sunglasses, backpacks and carrying cases; the sides of school buses; the front page of the Sunday magazine section in the newspaper; the plastic bags in which newspapers are home-delivered; shopping carts in supermarkets; the backs of theater tickets; and page edges of phone books; to name a few I've noticed. Ads targeted at youth are heard on Channel One in thousands of high schools every morning. Channel One's ads, according to Barber, sell at rates that rival those of a Super Bowl broadcast. More advertising is heard on public radio than was formerly the case, and product endorsements appear within movies.

The boundaries of ethics and even legality are being pushed by word-of-mouth marketing, also called viral advertising or buzz marketing. Students at some colleges are paid by software companies to promote their products by mentioning them to other students. Each time a friend downloads the product, the student who recommended it makes money. Housewives are paid to talk up household and personal care products to their friends. These "brand ambassadors" are not required to disclose that they are making money by promoting a certain product.

The biggest player in the word-of-mouth marketing industry is Procter & Gamble. The company has 225,000 teenagers involved in a program called Tremor; another program, Vocalpoint, has enlisted over 500,000 moms. Vocalpoint mothers were given a new kind of dishwashing soap called "Dawn," and encouraged to casually work its name into chats with friends by talking about how hard it is to get kids to help with the dinner dishes. The campaign worked, reported P&G executive Steve Knox: "In that particular place, we nearly doubled Dawn's business—all through word of mouth."[4]

After being asked by a watchdog group to establish clear guidelines on word-of-mouth advertising, the Federal Trade Commission issued a staff opinion saying that there's nothing illegal about consumers expressing satisfaction. Even the Word of Mouth Marketing Association, which purports to regulate this segment of the industry, does not account for such power differentials as teachers marketing to students or bosses to employees. Advertising analyst Peter Kim says the close relationships that buzz marketing depends on makes enforcement virtually impossible.[5] The ethical question remains unanswered.

"The [advertising] industry's implicit message," writes Gary Ruskin, executive director of Commercial Alert (a nonprofit consumer watchdog organization), "is a total lack of respect for our time, our privacy, our attention, our peace of mind, and not least for our concerns about our kids."[6]

Companies spend huge sums of money to buy naming rights for large public concert and sports arenas. For example, the largest enclosed venue in Denver, site of the 2008 Democratic Convention, is known as the Pepsi Center. Thus every mention of the venue is an advertisement for a product, a substantial change from the former practice of naming large public buildings and sports venues for prominent local citizens.

Our mailboxes used to contain only letters from people or businesses with whom we had had some contact, as well as magazines we subscribed to, but now we find a fistful of junk mail, another way advertising invades our home. If we don't like this daily arrival of unwanted solicitations, it is up to us to take steps to stop it; the default is that it will continue. The San Francisco Department of the Environment tells us that 100 million trees must be cut down *every year* to produce America's 42 *billion* pieces of junk mail, with nationwide disposal costs at about $320 million.[7] Yet thousands of people, primarily postal workers and print shop employees, have come to depend on junk mail for their livelihood. A local legislator where I live sponsored an anti–junk mail bill but a short time later withdrew it, after a deluge of calls and e-mails from the many people who would have been put out of work if it passed. The issue is not a simple one to resolve.

The peace of our homes has been callously disregarded by telemarketers who call at mealtimes and just about any time, badgering us to buy, and there are still a few solicitors who go door to door in neighborhoods. Due to the profitability of advertising, citizens have had difficulty getting laws passed to curtail it; however, there is evidence that ordinary citizens are getting fed up. Finally, although it took years, a national no-call list was implemented, restricting allowable calls to charitable organizations and companies with whom the resident had done business previously. Another encouraging sign is from a 2004 Yankelovich poll in which thirty-three percent of respondents said they would be willing to accept a lower standard of living if it meant no more advertising and marketing.[8] The good news here is that a severe cutback on allowable advertising would *not* have to mean a lower standard of living. Beyond being comfortable and having enough, additional possessions and experiences are more likely to drain our finances and wellbeing than to enhance them.

The overconsumption promoted by advertising puts our environment at increasing risk, as natural resources are depleted for frivolous or disposable items, like fad clothing, party supplies, or single-use packaging. Fossil fuels are extracted and become countless plastic bags and cheap toys, purses, CDs; forests are cut down and turned into paper towels and napkins, the cleared land becoming grazing land for resource-intensive and obesity-promoting fast food burgers. Our rivers are polluted by fertilizer and pesticide runoff from cornfields grown, not for actual food, but for high-fructose corn syrup to make soft drinks, or for an unnatural diet for methane-producing cattle.

What is particularly alarming is that organizations promoting peaceful lifestyles that have raised the necessary funds to pay current rates for television advertising have had their ads rejected by the networks. Kalle Lasn, editor-in-chief of the Vancouver-based Adbusters Media Foundation, has tried for ten years to get anti-consumption ads broadcast, including ones encouraging the public to "Buy Nothing" on the Friday after Thanksgiving, and to question the consumption of fast food. Only CNN has broadcast his ads. When a reason for the rejection has been given, it is either that the media do not want to anger their corporate advertisers, on whom they are financially dependent, or that Lasn's ads constitute advocacy. He claims that ads for cars and fast food advocate certain lifestyles just as his ads do, and he wonders "why, while ads that show the negative effects of alcohol or smoking are accepted, those that depict the dangers of high-fat food are not."[9] It's not only the anti-consumption message that is not allowed to be broadcast: the United Church of Christ was refused by both CBS and NBC for an ad that promoted acceptance for gays and lesbians.[10]

Occasionally advertisements give us facts about products and services that are true and useful, but mostly they inflame our greed, glorify wealth, stimulate overspending and debt, promote the wasteful use of environmental resources, encourage and reinforce low self-esteem, and deceive us about the likely results of the purchase and use of products and services. None of these outcomes make us, or society as a whole, more peaceful. By removing our names from junk mail and telemarketing lists, reducing television watching, becoming more savvy about advertising's falsehoods, helping to educate others, especially children, about them, and by buying sensibly, we are doing what we can to counter advertising's harmful effects.

Chapter Seven

Media Saturation

Americans choose to spend more and more of their non-job time under the influence of media, whether it be watching television, surfing the Internet, or listening to the radio. A recent survey reported that the average amount of time a person spends with these three media is a whopping nine and a half hours per day![1] And some people, especially the younger people who responded to the survey, watch TV and the Internet at the same time (counted by the survey as double the amount of time). For the sake of this discussion, print media are being included along with broadcast media. What are we gaining by turning ourselves over to the opinions, entertainment and commercial solicitations of others for such a large chunk of our time? Or, more to the point, what are we losing? And what does all this watching and listening have to do with world peace?

We've just seen in the previous chapter the peace-destroying effects of advertising. In addition to badgering us to buy stuff, the media impact our health: physical, social and mental. Physically, we spend time sitting in front of the TV or computer that we could spend going for a walk around the neighborhood or taking a yoga class. Television watching and video game–playing has become a particular concern in the case of children and youth, whose health is compromised at an early age by sitting for many hours in front of a screen instead of being outside playing. In addition, both children and adults may be more likely to eat snacks while watching—foods that are usually not healthful and promote weight gain.

Children's social development may also suffer, as media watching is essentially a solitary activity, even if others are sitting in the same room watching with them. The social interaction involved in play or in talking face-to-face with others helps ground children in the real world and builds skills that are useful in school and later on in business. Adults too may begin to feel isolated if time they might otherwise spend socially is diverted to solitary TV watching or surfing the web.

Excessive media watching impacts mental health as well, just as we noted above in the case of advertising. Comparing oneself to people one sees in the media is unrealistic and can engender discouragement that otherwise would not arise. When the average woman sees gorgeous female bodies onscreen, presented as young and perfect in every detail, she may obsess about her own looks, developing a negative opinion of her own body and appearance, perhaps even to the point of depression. Because older women are not valued in the media the way young ones are, she may think that aging is ugly and may even succumb to ads for cosmetic surgery, which is painful, dangerous and expensive, possibly beyond her budget. In the same way, seeing superb performing artists who have spent years honing their skills may discourage the viewer from even beginning to explore her own creativity in vocal or instrumental music or dance, thinking, "I could never be that good." There is a subtle effect that leads to disparaging one's own abilities. Whereas, if the viewer compares herself with actual people she knows, her opinion of her potential talent is much higher.

This is not to say that we should avoid watching the beautiful and talented—not at all. Excellence in the arts can be deeply inspiring and should be supported. It is often such a thrilling performance or breathtaking work of art that first motivates us to try to develop our own talent. But being constantly bombarded by these images and performances for several hours a day at home and from magazine racks wherever one shops is too much. That, combined with restricted access to real people (because we work too hard, have too much to do, live too far away to visit friends and family very often) can warp one's self-esteem. Many images of models in magazines, thanks to the marvels of digital photo manipulation, appear more perfect than they actually are.

Another casualty of too much media consumption is our imagination. When we read a book, we have to fill in the scenes and imagine the characters in our minds, how they look and dress. We often have to construct what they might be thinking. The same is true when we tell or hear stories. But with movies, we are shown exactly what characters look like and see the locales where events take place. Again, this is not to suggest that we shouldn't ever watch movies, but that if we're always shown exactly how things are, we are unthinkingly accepting someone else's impressions (e.g., the movie's director or costume designer), and our imagination and critical thinking skills never get exercised. Over time this tends to make viewers more passive, less willing to trust their own instincts.

Then there is the aspect that is perhaps foremost in the minds of those who sponsor "Turn Off Your TV" week or similar events: the countless images of violence of every description. War, murder, rape, fighting, robbery, racism, revenge, suicide, on down to hurtful speech, lying and betrayal can be seen any day of the week. By age eighteen, the average young person has seen 200,000 acts of violence, including 40,000 murders.

We who aspire to be practical peacemakers would be wise to avoid watching or listening to violence in the media. If violent scenes are casually watched, whether as news or entertainment, we come away feeling powerless, depressed, persuaded that the world is more hostile than it actually is, and that most people act solely out of self-interest, not caring who gets hurt. Or, on the other hand, we may be influenced to believe that violence is the most effective way to settle a dispute, or that there is heroism in killing. In either case, it is highly counterproductive to our commitment to furthering peace in ourselves and the world.

That said, there may be occasions when the watching of violence gives us necessary knowledge about an issue. For example, before I began going out into the community to promote vegetarianism, I watched film footage of actual slaughterhouse operations. This served two purposes: the gut-wrenching horror of it kept me motivated to continue the outreach, and when I was asked a question about animal slaughter—high school students especially are curious about the gory details—I was able to answer accurately. Even in the service of our activism, however, we are wise not to overdo the watching of violence lest we become depressed or desensitized.

In my own life, I experienced some months of frequent insomnia. I'd miss two hours or more of sleep at night, drag through my workday, and feel too tired at the end of it to do anything in the evening. I had no particular worries personally, so I began to notice what I thought about when I was unable to sleep. It was mostly the people and events I'd read about in the news—I was worrying and grieving for people I'd never met and whose difficulties I could do virtually nothing about (except perhaps giving to charity, which I was already doing). I would agonize about our government's policies. My heart would go out to victims of disease or war. I would frequently read of motor vehicle accidents, coverage of which makes it look like about ninety percent of drivers are careless and unsafe. I would read about accidental deaths, like being struck by lightning, and worry about that, even though the odds of being struck are extremely small.

Finally I realized that to be able to sleep I was going to have to restrict how much of this murder and mayhem I took in. I limited myself to reading the online news once a week, and discovered it had become something of an addiction—I really missed knowing what was going on every day. The important thing to keep in mind regarding "what is going on" as the media report it is that stories that make the news are stories that are unusual or rare. So the violent, shocking, repugnant acts that some humans commit are a tiny minority of all human acts, and ordinary and even kind acts are the vast majority of what is actually happening. Freak accidents and destructive storms are rare as well. Most people act and drive responsibly; care about their families, friends and companion animals; are honest; in general, do very little harm to each other. Nearly all people go through their day without encountering extreme weather conditions.

Yet to read or listen to the news fills one's mind with parents who murder their children, troubled youth who torture cats, suicide bombers, earthquakes or hurricanes that destroy whole cities, and so on.

Another result of the prevalence of media consumption is the increase in what I'll call public noise. The media give us a constant barrage of music playing and people talking. In bygone generations, people never heard or saw strangers revealing their most intimate misbehaviors, or expressing angry and strident political opinions. They heard only the voices of actual people in their lives. When they went to buy something in a store, eat in a restaurant, or visit a doctor or dentist's office, it was quiet, whereas now we have to hear nonstop playing of soft rock or oldies, sometimes even with commercials. At a music store, we may have our ears blasted with hard rock from the minute we walk in until we leave, even if what we went there to buy was relaxing meditation music. Even if we minimize noise in our own households, we may not be able to avoid hearing music playing or people talking on our neighbors' or coworkers' media players. The loss of public quiet increases stress and scatteredness, shortens tempers, and interferes with calm thinking.

We need to be aware that media news is geared toward ratings, not toward balanced reporting. In the early days of television, stations were required by the FCC to devote a portion of their programming to public service, and broadcasting the news fulfilled this requirement. Now news is much closer to entertainment than to a balanced reporting of what is happening. Sensational events like murder trials and sex scandals are given much more coverage than is justified, while news that we really need to know, like global warming, species extinction and the truth about Iraq, is often minimized or excluded.

Once I limited my news intake to once a week, I was amazed at how quickly my sleeping patterns improved. When the only drivers in my experience were the ones I encountered in real life, I was astonished at how much their driving skills had improved! When the only people I encountered were the ones in real life, I discovered that nearly all of them are helpful and want to do the right thing. Do I miss hearing about some important events? Absolutely. But if such events are important enough, I figure that someone will tell me. And the increased peace of mind I feel is more than worth anything I might miss.

We can make an exception about keeping up with candidates and issues on which we will eventually need to vote. We may want to protest, write letters, and in other ways try to influence public opinion, and must be informed to do so. By scanning headlines in print or online news sources, we can read just those stories that will keep us current.

We may form inaccurate perceptions when we buy into the world that the media present, but at least we have our own life experience as a reality check. However, American television shows and films are seen all over the globe, and viewers elsewhere have no way to judge these distortions. Viewers in other countries may think the majority of us belong to the superrich or cheat on our spouses or rob banks or kill policemen or, at the very least, are silly and stupid. These false impressions may lead to envy of our riches, contempt for our superficiality and wastefulness, or outrage at our immorality, all of which are breeding grounds for hatred and violence toward us.

So, to answer our question from the beginning of this chapter: How does our consumption of media affect world peace? We have only to review the personal qualities that the media tend to reinforce: greed, physical inactivity, isolation, the dulling of our imagination and ability to think for ourselves, agitation, unrealistic anxiety, short attention span, oversimplification of complex issues, stunted social development and poor health in children, and the perception that violence is commonplace—in a word, disempowerment. Do these sound like the attributes of a calm person, positive about themselves and their world, capable of peaceful living? Does this view of the world encourage a closing of the gap between the superrich and the desperately poor? Does this view make us better understood abroad? How much television and radio programming, news and magazine reading will you take in today? The choice is yours.

Chapter Eight

Rudeness

Our need to cram the greatest number of activities, whether they are truly worth doing or not, into the least amount of time has shifted the civility of our social interactions a considerable distance along the spectrum from courtesy toward rudeness. Even though the courteous response often takes no more time, we become so focused on our self-appointed goals, of getting all our errands done, that we lose our ability to relate to others, even those others we see regularly.

If we want to be peaceful ourselves and by our actions encourage peaceful responses in others, we need to take a serious look at societal courtesy and how we can help strengthen it. Courtesy is thinking of others—what they need and want, how to make them feel better about themselves and how to help lift any dark moods. We do this by taking the time to listen carefully both to what they are saying and, to the best of our ability, what they are not saying. We can often ease awkward situations by paying this kind of attention and by careful listening.

In our present society, many kinds of social comfort and courtesy have fallen by the wayside; we are all the poorer for it. Lest this chapter sound like I have become stuck in the 1950s or '60s, I want to reassure readers that I wouldn't want to return to those days, or to turn away from the technology, medical breakthroughs, and improvement in the status of women and minorities that we enjoy today. I call for a thoughtful consideration of old-fashioned courtesy, for the purpose of bringing it forward into the twenty-first century to create and maintain a peaceful and supportive social milieu. My describing boorish behavior is not to judge, but to outline clearly what we have lost so it can be restored.

I can remember a time, and I am not yet eligible for senior discounts, when families routinely ate together and, before beginning, returned thanks in some fashion for the food on the table. No one began eating until all were served. Dishes that were out of reach were requested by asking, "Will you please pass the _____?" Conversational topics that were unpleasant were avoided or postponed, and people did not talk with a mouthful of food or interrupt anyone else. Whoever had cooked the food was complimented on it. No phone calls from solicitors intruded, nor would anyone have answered a pager or taken a personal call at the table had that technology existed. Anyone needing to leave the table early was expected to ask, "Will you excuse me?" They would usually state the reason, rise and push their chair back up to the table. Have you eaten a family dinner like this any time in the last twenty years? If so, you are in the minority.

I recall an instance a few years ago when my husband and I invited two friends to dinner at our home. During the meal, one friend's cell phone rang; he answered it and proceeded to talk to the caller without excusing himself or even getting up from the table. He took out a small notebook and starting making notes at the table! After a while, he did get up and walk away from the table, but continued the call to the end without suggesting to the caller that it was an inappropriate time and offering to call back. When he returned to the table, he made no comment or excuse, as though his behavior was completely acceptable.

Except in an emergency, does anyone really need to take calls during a meal? A meal lasts probably a half-hour, perhaps an hour with a group in a restaurant, and preserving that time together uninterrupted can greatly increase our satisfaction and feelings of peace and harmony. Try it as an experiment with your friends or family. Notice how you feel when everyone's attention remains on each other throughout the meal, and at some other time have a meal with everyone coming and going at different times, taking calls, and so forth. Which do you prefer?

Formerly, no one could talk on the phone while driving, nor was there as much eating while driving. Drivers whose attention was on the road could be much more aware of pedestrians and cyclists than can the distracted drivers we have today. No one was doing the large amount of driving that many are today, which can dull the attention of even the best drivers.

I am astounded that some people want to have phones on their ears every moment, even making calls while walking the dog on a beautiful morning. As we wean ourselves to a less intense need to answer every call, we won't need to take or make phone calls in traffic, and that will improve our driving skills. Injury from vehicle accidents is not as large a risk to our health as are diseases of affluence, but nonetheless it would reduce our health care costs if we could drive more safely.

In the past, workers were expected to give attention to one task at a time instead of being required to handle three or four simultaneously. Extending courtesy to a customer or client is extremely difficult if the worker is trying to do more than one thing at once. Such multi-tasking has often been necessitated by staffing cuts, in which unfilled positions are allowed to remain unfilled, and thus fewer workers handle the same, or an increasing, workload. Just try to find one of the few remaining salespersons for help in a retail environment! From an occasional annoying and frustrating necessity, multi-tasking has become increasingly acceptable, then expected, and its pace intensified. That is, the ability and willingness to habitually limit service to one person in order to accommodate another, to risk error on one person's account or product in order to handle several others' accounts, is now highly sought after and in fact a deal-breaking job requirement. Yet, according to Gary Small, M.D., professor of psychiatry and biobehavioral sciences at the UCLA Center on Aging, multi-tasking can lead to more problems than it supposedly solves because it tends to confuse one's focus. "Multi-tasking," he says, "is not good for memory." It also, in the case of texting while walking, can be hazardous to one's health, as ambulatory texters on busy city streets run into walls, poles, doorways, parked cars, other people, or even fall down stairs.[1] Such texters are more prone to facial injuries than an average person falling because, holding their devices close to their faces, their hands are not as available to break their falls.

I can remember a time when no employee who serves the public would show up for work in wrinkled clothes, ragged or torn jeans, short shorts or wet hair. Punctuality was expected. Workers did not eat or drink in the work area. Workers serving the public did not have to deal with customers talking on cell phones while the worker was trying to serve them.

Women, and especially teenage girls, rarely appeared in ordinary daytime public places wearing tight clothes revealing deep cleavage and exposed bellies, as they do now. In dressing this way, they seem to encourage being viewed as sex objects, and to increase the likelihood of (presumably) unwanted sexual advances. Exploitation and unresolved sexual tension can be precursors to violence. And then there are multiple body piercings, another formerly unknown blight on the social landscape. I mention multiple piercings, particularly noticeable on tongues and lips, where they interfere with eating and speaking, because they communicate self-mutilation and a reminder of deliberately chosen pain and violence. Extensive tattoos are another example of self-inflicted pain that, like multiple piercings, have inexplicably become fashion statements, not only for confused and rebellious youth but for some older people as well. The rudeness in it is that those who want to objectify through their dress or inflict pain on themselves in order to display and decorate their bodies reinforce, even glorify, images of violence which the rest of us cannot avoid when we encounter them.

The noise level of our public places has increased noticeably, bringing with it disruption, stress, irritation, and loss of sleep. Not too long ago, lawn mowing services and others who work outdoors in neighborhoods did not start noisy equipment early in the morning unless it was an emergency. Now, however, the sound of large mowers routinely begins on summer mornings around 7:45 A.M., right outside one's window. Anyone needing to sleep beyond that time or enjoy quiet in the early morning can forget it. The workplace and retail environment formerly had no radios blaring rock or rap or talk show callers filled with anger; lately, I even heard noisy radio over the speakers in a dental office. Previously, parents with misbehaving young children took them out of public places so as not to disturb others.

The inappropriate use of cell phones, mentioned above as a cause of interruptions and distractions, warrants another mention here for the noise involved. People nearly always talk louder on a cell phone than they would to someone present beside them. If we are near someone talking on a cell phone—which could be in the quiet of a park or museum, doing our grocery shopping, in the library, waiting for or traveling on a bus, or just walking down the street—we can avoid neither the noise nor the unwanted eavesdropping we're forced to do. All of these places were formerly free of conversation except for people talking quietly to their companions. Let me make myself clear: not cell phones in themselves, but the inconsiderate ways people use them, are the problem. I enjoy going to see IMAX movies, so I've heard many times the announcement that is made before the film begins. The audience is asked twice to turn off all cell phones and pagers, and parents are asked to remove from the theater any children who become disruptive. These two reminders should just be common sense, but in today's society courteous behavior cannot be assumed.

The rarely mentioned casualty of all this noise is silence.

Silence has a calming influence. It is healing, prevents stress and possible hearing loss, and helps people get along better. Whenever I've attended a silent retreat or been out in nature for a period of time, I've been able to let go of stress, focus on what's really important, and better appreciate my surroundings and the food I eat. Silence opens our hearts and nurtures our creativity. The damage people do to each other by careless speech, although sometimes subtle, is considerable. Quieting our background noise, including cutting back substantially on public cell phone conversations, would encourage people to think, to appreciate each other more and be more likely to say only what is appropriate and strengthens the friendship.

A commonplace discourtesy experienced by hosts of dinners, receptions and other events is the failure of invited guests to RSVP. This increases the stress for the event's planners because they then cannot determine how much food and drink to purchase, how many party supplies, and how much seating and table space will be needed. In the old days, an RSVP was expected whether the person planned to attend or not. Although it was a nice touch to receive the good wishes of those who couldn't make it, the only people we really need to hear from are the ones who plan to attend. Yet now even that is unreliable. I don't do much entertaining, but in my limited experience of organizing dinner parties, I've had friends fail to let me know they were coming—I wait and wait and then perhaps contact them at the last minute.

I've occasionally had people who had said they were coming, cancel the day before or day of the event without any illness or emergency as an excuse. Social gatherings strengthen community, giving people a chance to begin or re-energize friendships and join together in mutual support. Outgoing people who enjoy entertaining are important resources for community wellbeing, yet the cavalier attitude displayed by many guests about responding can take the fun out of hosting a gathering. Hosts may decide not to entertain again. Sending a phone or e-mail response to an invitation takes very little time, and is something everyone can do to strengthen the fabric of community.

In times past, if someone wanted to own a particular music recording, they bought it. Technology has increased our access to copyrighted content, but unfortunately our ethics as a society have fallen short. Now it is not unusual for someone to go to the public library, check out the maximum number of music CDs, return them the next day, and check out the maximum number again, return them the next day, and so forth. It is not just a suspicion that the borrowers are burning copies at home for personal use; some people have even thanked the library for allowing them to build up their music collections! Others try to get free downloads. Any possible obligation to support the musicians, whose countless hours of practice and effort the borrower enjoys and wants to own, has been forgotten. Songs have changed, too. Formerly, any offensive lyrics were mumbled or slurred so that only those in the know realized what was being said. Now song lyrics are more easily understood and include not only sexually explicit but violent content so graphic that many popular youth-oriented CDs carry parental advisory warning labels.

Reflecting on the many kinds of rudeness that society now seems willing to tolerate brings to mind a bumper sticker slogan: "If you're not completely appalled, you haven't been paying attention." Although probably intended as a comment on national politics, it applies to social behavior as well. I've often been appalled, but that by itself isn't the solution. By acting courteously, in ways that are thoughtful of others, we do what we can to restore graciousness to our social relationships. By encouraging people to gather, we help counteract the isolation many people feel.

Affluence allows those who prefer to live alone to do so. This is beneficial up to a point—no one wants to live with someone incompatible. However, in the U.S. today, over a quarter of all households are single-person occupied.[2] Until these last few decades, no society at any time in history had large numbers of people living alone. Previously, it was necessary for economic reasons, and often for basic survival, for people to live in tribal or family groups. People living alone can do whatever they want, whenever they want, without considering anyone else's needs or preferences. Such people, if they don't get plenty of other social contact, may begin to lose their ability to pay attention in conversation, to feel comfortable with the give and take of social interaction, and to defer their own gratification occasionally in order to be loving to another. I believe long-term living alone was probably a major factor in our dinner guest's cell phone use, mentioned above.

Thinking about this leads to the question of which comes first: Does selfishness and rudeness arise because so many of us are living alone, or are we living alone because those we've tried living with have been rude and selfish? Clearly we all need to put others first more of the time, although not to the extent of denying our own legitimate needs, as particularly women have been tragically taught in the past. All of the discourtesies recounted above can be prevented by cultivating thoughtfulness and present-moment awareness. When we are tempted to slight others, we can remind ourselves how we would feel if we were the other person. Reducing our busyness will also help immeasurably. As we slow down, learn and practice considering others' interests, listening to them, and being gracious to them, our definition of "others" expands and expands, eventually to include all beings, animate and inanimate. Our personal kindness and patience, and that of the recipients of our actions who pass it on, benefit the entire planet and all who share it with us.

⌐ Chapter Nine ⌐

Prejudice

Throughout history, humans have tended to believe that people who look like themselves, think like themselves, worship the same deities, and have the same language and culture, are to be trusted, supported and defended. This mindset further justifies treating people who are different as harshly as may be necessary to further the interests of one's own group. The more different the others are, the less worthy of respect they are thought to be.

Earlier in human history, when our population was low and people usually lived their whole lives within a small tribe, this belief may have had some survival value. We've always been more likely to trust the people we know well, and at this early time the people we knew well would all have been members of our tribe. Anyone outside our tribe who showed up was unlikely to propose cooperation or peaceful interaction; they probably wanted to take food, land, women, children or animals. At best, they would steal; at worst, they would kill some of us to get what they wanted.

In this context, perhaps our fear and hatred of people who were different had some realistic value.

Our social encounters have, of course, changed dramatically. Now, especially in our big cities, we rub elbows with people from many cultures every day. The person at the next desk in our office may be from another continent. In my work, I hear several different languages spoken in the course of a day. We see people from every region of the world in every possible public context. Our children go to school with kids of all races and beliefs. Our next-door neighbor may be of a different sexual orientation than we are. Our everyday household goods are made halfway around the globe. It is time, and past time, to let go of this notion that people of different cultures, ethnic backgrounds and lifestyles are to be viewed with suspicion and treated with distrust. Yet our prejudices endure.

That these prejudices have been the cause of massive violence and untold suffering throughout human history is unassailably true. The brutal mass killings in Tibet, Cambodia and Rwanda come to mind, among numerous other examples that could be mentioned. Once we depersonalize other groups in our thinking and speaking, we enable torture, exile or genocide of these peoples to happen, and happen they have, over and over again. Less immediately disruptive are the kinds of institutionalized violence that kill not the body but the soul. The denial of respect, adequate education, jobs, housing, healthful food, a clean environment, the right to vote, and in some cases even basic freedoms breeds yet more violence. The targeted group may be denied access to the rest of society.

To tackle prejudice, we need to examine why groups have had the need to put down those who differ. Of what are they/ we afraid? Is it really in the dominant group's best interests to grab all the goodies, or does such greed create an underclass that will eventually bring down those in power? People believe that there is a shortage of natural and economic resources, but would that be true if we took only what we need? What would society look like if we treated everyone equally? These are age-old questions, but become more urgent in our time as more countries acquire world-destroying weapons, and as population soars.

Everyone who harbors even the slightest wish for world peace needs to drop the notion that his or her own way is the only right way to behave or believe, or that his or her group is somehow special or superior as a people. In that basic mistake, repeated over and over down through history, is where mass violence truly begins. One theory for the belief in group superiority is that by conquering their neighbors, a tribe's members diminish their own fear of death, their fear of personal and cultural extinction. It is somehow overlooked that a group need not conquer others in order to prevent cultural extinction; cultures can survive quite well by living peacefully side by side with other cultures. And they can do better than just survive; they can actually be enriched if they share wisdom and practical skills with their neighbors.

Although shortsighted and dangerous, it is unfortunately easy to believe one's own group is the best and somehow has the "right" to subjugate another group. We've seen this in our own history, for example, through the belief in "manifest destiny," which held that European settlers and their descendants were the rightful conquerors of the entire American West. This led inevitably to the genocide of native Americans, and to their lands' natural resources being shamelessly squandered. Especially now when population pressures are increasing, isn't it time for humans to stop stealing and destroying lands and impoverishing peoples just because we can? Like any other belief, this one can be changed. It is possible, if we truly want peace and want to see every child fed, to renounce our prejudices and scale back our wasteful consumption, but it will take commitment and daily practice.

That practice will include such actions as putting a little less on our dinner plate and replacing animal foods with plant foods, thinking carefully before we buy anything we don't really need, choosing mindfully what entertainment we will take in, learning to watch our thinking so that when a prejudicial thought pops up we won't just accept and reinforce it, speaking and listening carefully and lovingly so as not to water the seeds of neglect, anger or greed in ourselves or others. As much as possible, we will need to select other peaceful people as companions and friends, ideally others who are practicing with us.

Each of us desperately needs to let go of the mindset that our own religion is the only correct one, that other people who worship differently are a threat to our wellbeing. By believing that these others are destined for eternal punishment anyway, or are not fully human, the dominant group has justified killing them. The Inquisition happened centuries ago, the Holocaust decades ago, but many of us still carry vestiges of that kind of thinking, perhaps not that we think the "infidels" or "inferior race" should be tortured and killed, but yet believing that they are wrong or flawed and that they don't deserve to be treated as equals. Any thought of "them" as being less deserving than "us" is a violent thought; violence appears first in our thinking. Jesus makes this point in the Sermon on the Mount when he goes beyond the commandment "Thou shalt not kill" to say that even to be angry with one's brother is to be liable to judgment (Matt. 5:21–22).

How can we work to free the human race from such a destructive worldview? First, we can learn to communicate better. In the U.S. our common language is English, so English holds by far the best possibility for understanding each other. To support and further the ability of everyone to speak a common language, we need to make sure that ESL classes are widely available, low-cost or free, and easy for recently arrived people to access. If we have time we can volunteer to teach such classes. We can cast our vote for public funds to be made available for this purpose. We can also be patient when speaking to a person struggling with the English language. We may need to set up rewards for non-English speakers who learn English and demonstrate proficiency in it.

Second, we can pay close attention when the tendency arises to categorize people of a different group. If we reflect on how inaccurate it would be to lump everyone in our *own* religion or race together as having certain characteristics, we can perhaps better understand why stereotypes of large groups of people are both false and insulting. Saying, "They're all like that," whatever "that" may refer to in a particular conversation, can never be a step toward peace and understanding. Instead, it draws listeners into a deeper feeling of separation from, and perhaps suspicion about, the group being discussed. Such careless, even dangerous, talk exacerbates the confusion and covert hostility in the group doing the talking.

If we set our course in this direction of nondiscrimination and peace, it scarcely matters that we will fall short of our goal time and time again. We just renew our commitment to the practice of peace and go forward without self-recrimination. We can help ourselves by frequently reflecting on peace and strengthening our aspiration toward it. Contemplate, for example, a world in which no family would grieve for a son lost in battle, no child would be orphaned by terrorism or war. Think of all the beneficial ways the huge sums of money now spent on "defense" could be spent toward better education and living conditions for all. Imagine more and more lands set aside for forests and other natural wildlife habitat. In such ways we can refresh our commitment to acting peacefully instead of selfishly.

Churches and other spiritual or religious organizations can inspire, encourage and support their members in following a daily path toward simpler living and compassion. Leaders of these organizations can offer classes and study groups on a variety of topics, such as these:

- Effective communication, including nonviolent conflict resolution;
- Meditation and slowing our hectic pace;
- Resisting the message of greed in advertising and other media programming;
- Recognizing prejudice and chauvinistic attitudes, understanding the damage these attitudes can cause, and overcoming them;
- Distinguishing wants from needs;
- Reducing our environmental footprint; and
- Studies in comparative religion.

These topics can be made fun and interesting

in a variety of ways:

- Role playing;
- Incorporating food by demonstrating easy vegetarian cooking from another culture along with an appreciation of that culture;
- Making a collage of magazine pages containing misleading advertising;
- Encouraging group members to report their successes in making specific changes; and
- Discussing relevant readings from current news.

There already exist discussion group curricula on such topics; for example, those published by the Northwest Earth Institute. If these kinds of topics are not being addressed in religious and spiritual congregations, members need to take the lead and demand such training and practice.

Eventually, it becomes easier to see each person, no matter how different from us in appearance or belief, as part of our family and to want the same peace and comfort for him or her as we would want for our own family members. The Dalai Lama reminds us, when we see those we perceive as very different, to keep in mind what we all have in common: that every sentient being wants to be happy and free from suffering. The more we practice, the more our hearts will open, and the more likely we will be to think and act peacefully.

Chapter Ten

Environmental Degradation

We can never be at peace on this planet until we all respect it enough to use its resources wisely. The disease and hardship that result when resources become scarce or polluted cause poverty and resentment that will always lead to conflict. Degradation and species extinction may become irreversible. Once again, the heart of the problem lies in the lifestyle of affluence.

Now that Al Gore and others have justifiably drawn attention to it, global warming seems to be the environmental issue foremost in the public mind, and it is indeed one of the most threatening. It has become well known that the burning of huge amounts of fossil fuels is filling our atmosphere with carbon dioxide, warming the earth's surface to the point where our ability to sustain ourselves is endangered. Most people probably think that the use of fossil fuels for transportation is the greatest contributor to the problem. But that is not so, according to the Food and Agriculture

Organization (FAO) of the United Nations: the answer lies on our dinner plates, if meat is what's for dinner. The raising of cattle and other livestock generates more greenhouse gas emissions as measured in CO_2 equivalent—eighteen percent—than all transportation combined, because of the methane it produces. Methane is a gas that is twenty-three times as warming as CO_2.[1]

Livestock accounts for thirty-seven percent of all human-induced methane and sixty-four percent of ammonia, which contributes significantly to acid rain. Furthermore, it generates sixty-five percent of human-related nitrous oxide, which has an astonishing 296 times the Global Warming Potential (GWP) of CO_2. It is also a major source of land and water degradation, and uses thirty percent of the earth's entire land surface.

Our ability to grow food is more fragile than we might think, in that a few degrees' variation in temperature can alter the growing cycle and the interaction of pests and predators to the point that a crop may not mature. The melting of polar ice caps could flood coastlines, causing huge upheavals of coastal populations, and endanger the continued flow of the warming Gulf Stream waters. Possible food shortages and disruptions of livelihood would inevitably lead to conflicts worldwide. What practical steps can we take to prevent these calamities and promote peace?

We know what we can do about the methane produced by cattle: stop eating meat and encourage others to do likewise.

What about the global warming gases that come from fuel burned for transportation and heating of buildings? We need to open our minds and hearts to understand that, because the planet's ability to clean the air is limited, we must change such habits as driving alone in a gas-guzzling vehicle several miles to pick up some trivial item. Limiting and combining trips will help, as will using a more efficient or alternative vehicle. We need to insulate our homes as much as we can, keep the temperatures in our homes a few degrees colder in winter and hotter in summer than we might prefer. We need to move, if necessary, to be closer to where we work, or at least closer to the public transportation that can get us there. Ideally we would be close enough to bike or walk most days, or be able to work from home. Although driving less wouldn't mean having to forego all pleasure trips, we certainly need to think carefully about our leisure travel and not just pick up and go on a whim. For example, if we want to drive fifty miles or more just to go hiking or to the beach, we cannot, as practical peacemakers, do that every weekend. Alternatives would be a closer location to hike, carpooling with others so that fewer vehicles go, or choosing an area we want to explore and then staying there for several days, rather than driving back and forth. Even if we drive a zero-polluting vehicle, we will still want to restrict our driving, so that our farmland and wildlife habitats are not increasingly paved over.

We also must seriously decrease our air travel, especially frivolous travel. In many countries, it's the fastest-growing single source of greenhouse gas emissions. A single long-haul flight can emit more carbon per passenger than months of SUV driving, and the carbon emitted at high altitudes appears to have a greater warming effect than the same amount of carbon emitted on the ground by cars and factories. According to the UK activist group Plane Stupid, "We could close every factory, lock away every car and turn off every light in the country, but it won't halt global warming if we keep taking planes as often as we do."[2] Unlike for cars, there is at present no cleaner alternative fuel or more efficient engine likely for planes. Some travelers try to make their flights carbon neutral by donating to a forestry project; airlines and travel agents are beginning to offer such options. It is unlikely, however, that carbon offsets can ever compensate for the damage. My personal response is to take no more than one plane trip per year, which is to visit family 1,100 miles away. Those whose jobs require frequent air travel are in a difficult situation; changing jobs is never as easy as changing personal behavior patterns. Perhaps informed employees can find ways to point out to their supervisors the climate impact of air travel, and suggest replacing most trips with teleconferencing. It is my hope that greater awareness of the environmental impact of air travel will result in far fewer business trips being deemed necessary.

We can also reduce our ecological footprint by downsizing to a smaller home. Once we get rid of unnecessary possessions, a smaller space may be more workable than we would initially think. Just living in a smaller space and using less fuel for heat is making a difference, doing our part to prevent global warming. If we own our home, we can then get the smaller home better insulated and install solar panels. We need to think carefully about all kinds of renewable energy sources and take action as soon as we can. If enough people begin to live this way individually, there will develop a public will to see that commercial buildings and new construction are designed and built with minimal fuel consumption in mind. As more of us live in smaller homes, more densely populated neighborhoods, such as those built before the 1940s, will re-establish themselves, reducing driving distances and keeping more open land for wildlife habitat. Denser neighborhoods might eventually mean that CSAs (Community Supported Agriculture farms) could be closer in to the cities, so that fresh, locally grown food would not have to be transported as far as it currently does.

Less use of fossil fuels for driving and heating has, in addition to its beneficial effect on global warming, other positive impacts that will be much more readily apparent. One is the reduction of air pollution in our cities. Regardless of which pollutants from fuel burning seem to be prominent at a given time, "it's always something." Where I live we get ozone warnings in the summer—that is, unhealthfully high concentrations of ozone along the ground (not to be confused with the beneficial ozone high up in the stratosphere). This ozone in our breathing space can cause or exacerbate a variety of human respiratory ailments and damage trees and other plants, making them vulnerable to disease and insects. The biggest emitter of ozone-promoting VOCs (volatile organic compounds) along Colorado's Front Range where I live is oil and gas drilling. Thus a reduced demand for these fuels will result in less drilling and less ozone.

A common summertime activity, often connected with ozone alerts by the news media, is the use of gasoline-powered lawn mowers. Simple living in denser neighborhoods will greatly reduce the problem by encouraging people to convert expanses of lawn into food-producing gardens and by placing homes closer together so that the yard space needing maintenance is smaller. Gasoline mowers themselves can be replaced quite effectively by solar electric-powered mowers, or, for smaller lawns, push mowers.

Another benefit of cutting fuel usage by reducing driving will be more time spent in neighborhoods instead of feeling the need to escape. This additional time will improve relationships among neighbors, leading to caring more about the neighborhood and the desire to report problems and pick up litter. Litter-free streets will promote harmony and feed back into increased pride in keeping the area neat and clean. Lower fuel usage will also protect wildlife and keep the oceans cleaner by reducing the likelihood of oil spills, and protect the wellbeing of forests and urban trees, thus strengthening their air-cleaning abilities.

Factories are major users of fossil fuels to manufacture cars, appliances, furniture and other household goods, clothing, computers and every kind of physical possession we have. Many of these factories are overseas now instead of being located in the United States, which makes their global warming impact much worse, because it adds fuel for transworld transportation onto fuel for manufacturing usage. Furthermore, pollution requirements may not be as strict in the manufacturing countries as they are in the U.S. The practical response we can make is to buy fewer items, get as many of them secondhand as we can, and keep them in use longer before replacing them.

We must also—and here's the part we especially don't like to hear—be willing to pay more for each item, so that using fewer items does not put people out of work. For buyers, however, the additional expense per item is balanced out by our using fewer items, so it shouldn't make our cost of living that much higher. The willingness to pay more will mean managers of factories and farms can pay their workers more, and will not be under so much cost pressure to hire illegal immigrants for the lowest possible wages. Higher wages will make these jobs attractive to workers who plan to settle and raise their families in the U.S. Fewer illegal immigrants will ease current pressures on social services. Plus consumers will save on gasoline and heating fuels as we increase our efficiency, and on food costs.

How will we save on food? A vegetarian diet of vegetables, legumes, grains, nuts and fruit is delicious and promotes maximum human health, as we saw in Chapter One. We'll save when we buy these whole foods, as they are less expensive than processed foods. For example, think about the cost of a five-pound bag of potatoes and how long that would sustain you, compared to the similar cost of a bag of potato chips and how long that would sustain you. We usually save at the checkout counter when buying plant foods as compared to animal foods, although the substantial subsidies our government provides to support livestock agriculture can sometimes blur this price difference. And we save again in medical bills, by not developing the diseases of affluence—heart disease, cancer, obesity, and diabetes— nearly as much.

We can cultivate our desire to protect and nurture the planet by spending time in nature. If we can take public transportation to the mountains or the beach, or bicycle to trails, so much the better. We needn't drive long distances, however; our backyards, or walks through the neighborhood or nearby parks, can also serve. We can encourage children to play outside, to care for a companion animal or for a few plants in a garden, a windowsill, or a sprouter. We can involve families in growing vegetables and savoring their just-picked taste. If our city has public gardens, we can visit them more often. We can watch clouds, sunrises and sunsets, the moon and stars, and visit an observatory if possible for a closer look. We can pay attention to urban wildlife, such as squirrels, songbirds, bees, ducks and geese, and the life cycle of trees and other plants. We can occasionally go for a walk in the rain or snow.

Henry David Thoreau, considering the "luxury" of standing up to one's chin in a swamp for a whole day to better observe wildlife, commented, "Cold and damp—are they not as rich an experience as warmth and dryness?"[3] I use this remark as a joke with friends, but there is truth in it. I have discovered that by biking to work I am much more in tune with the weather and have a greater knowledge of the landscape of my neighborhood.

The suggestions given above will not only help the environment, but can have auxiliary benefits of more closeness and sharing between people, better health, more free time and more peaceful minds. However, our having been able for so long to consume so much has made conservation a hard sell. Most people don't like to hear anyone suggest that we practice restraint in the number of miles we drive or fly, be required by law to drive more efficient vehicles, purchase fewer consumer goods, or eat different foods. Until we can get the majority of the populace behind us, we must practice individually and consistently, without sitting in judgment of our more wasteful neighbors, but without giving in to higher consumption levels either.

Chapter Eleven

Overpopulation

The earth's burgeoning population threatens to undo every other improvement we can make. Our world population has grown more since 1950 than it did in the last four million years. Even though the *rate* of increase has generally been declining, the absolute numbers continue to go up sharply. World population is expected to reach 7.9 billion by 2025 and 9.1 billion by 2050. Already, according to Bread for the World, a Christian hunger organization, one child dies every five seconds from hunger-related causes,[1] and 854 million people across the world are hungry.[2]

In the United States, population is increasing at the rate of 2.8 million people every year,[3] and carbon dioxide emissions in this country are currently at 19.8 metric tons per capita.[4] The greater the population, the more they consume, and the greater the rise in levels of CO_2 and other greenhouse gases. The Intergovernmental Panel on Climate Change has estimated that in order to stop global warming, emissions must fall to sixty percent below 1990 levels before 2050; yet in this same period, global population is expected to increase by thirty-seven percent.[5] Additional U.S. births cause more environmental damage than births in the Global South, as a U.S. citizen consumes thirty times as much as a citizen of India,[6] for example. If all people on earth were to share the world's resources equally, Americans would have to reduce their overall consumption by *eighty percent*.[7]

Simple living begins its healing of the population problem by reducing the consumption of the affluent, so that more food and distribution resources are freed up to feed the billions of people we already have. As we saw in Chapter One, simple living will also reduce our health care costs at home, so more medical supplies can be sent overseas, if we have the will to do so.

At a cursory glance, simple living might seem to *increase* the likelihood of more offspring, given that families will be stronger, and one parent will usually be able to stay home for child care. However, simple living will also increase our awareness of being part of a global community, so we will see more clearly that *all* additional children increase the burden on available resources. We will come to understand that the extraction of fossil fuel resources requires life-destroying violence, such as that from dangerous mining, air and water pollution, drilling and oil spills that destroy wildlife and weaken ecosystems, and waging war to have access to oil and gas fields. However, even if someday all our vehicles are powered and our buildings heated and cooled by renewable energy, we will still have to keep paving wider roads and building more homes and commercial buildings for the additional people. We will realize that the more we have to farm in order to feed greater numbers of people, the more we lose our topsoil, our forests and grasslands, and our species diversity, which affect the survival of all. We have only so much arable land. We will see that the more noise, congestion, and competition for scarce resources we must endure, the more likely conflict becomes.

Thoughtful people who care about peace will come to understand that overpopulation leads to violence, because the earth can only support a finite number of people. When limited resources are no longer sufficient to support everyone, people naturally fight to obtain them, leading to war and genocide. Our allowing ourselves to grieve over such wars and genocides will make us more committed to prevent such mass violence in the future. Those of us—the vast majority—whose ancestors came to North America as immigrants, may realize that overpopulation is a primary cause of immigration.

It is instructive to look at how the Cherokees in the southeastern United States viewed the first white settlers who encroached on their land. According to John Ehle, author of *Trail of Tears: The Rise and Fall of the Cherokee Nation*, the Cherokees were envious: these white people had a much lower infant mortality rate, thus larger families, and they were successful in acquiring more land by means of having more powerful weapons. What the Cherokees, who had lived sustainably in the same area for thousands of years, didn't yet understand was that having large families meant the whites always needed more land, and that need led them to develop powerful means of killing those who stood in their way.

When a country has more people than it can support, increasing numbers will move to other countries. The best-case scenario is to move for better opportunities in the new country, such as Mexican citizens coming into the U.S.; however, necessity dictates that such movements will often be a desperate response to a resource war or famine. While overpopulation leads to immigration, the opposite is also true: immigration leads to overpopulation. A country that has long been successful in keeping its population in line with its resources may be completely overwhelmed if there is an influx of refugees from elsewhere. Population beyond what can be supported may shift location, but the problem remains constant.

If we want to be practical peacemakers we will take care to restrict the size of our own families, and some of us—I'm one of them—will voluntarily have no children at all. We will support organizations that work to make contraception acceptable and available to greater numbers of people, particularly teens, because currently one-third of population growth in the world is the result of unwanted pregnancies. At the national level, we will need to establish ways to reward lowered reproduction, perhaps tax breaks or other incentives. According to the Population Connection, if the United States could attain the family size of Canada (1.5 children per woman), we could reduce our yearly 2.8 million population increase by over 600,000, and if we could attain the family size of Italy and Spain (1.3 children per woman), we could cut our population growth by half.[8] Living simply can free up more of us to become population educators, giving public talks to interested groups.

Our society and nearly all societies tend to be pronatalist; that is, to accept as a given that childrearing brings happiness to the parents and to society. (We'll discuss the unquestioned acceptance of this belief later in this chapter.) One way we can all have an influence, parents and non-parents alike, is to question, in our conversations with friends and associates, these socially ingrained pronatalist myths. Let's look at them one by one.

Myth #1: *By having children, a man or woman proves him/herself sexually potent and fertile, and thus worthy of admiration.* Here the error is a confusion of the body with the self. Sexual potency and fertility pertain only to one's body, and say nothing about one's character or talents.

Having a large number of children irresponsibly is certainly not admirable, but even if one provides well for all of them, large families can no longer be seen as admirable from an international or planetary perspective. The fertile couple may be considered successful from a biological standpoint— they've passed down their genes all right—but on our overcrowded planet, repeating this kind of success turns to tragedy in the long run.

Another way I have heard Myth #1 expressed is, "Having children is part of being a woman." It can be, but if giving birth is expected or considered desirable for *every* woman to experience repeatedly throughout the fertile decades of her life, we cannot have peace on earth. There are just too many women of reproductive age currently alive.

Myth #2: *Contraception is sinful or contrary to the will of God.* How can it be sinful to prevent the conception of children who will compete, and often die, struggling for available food supplies and health care? On the other end of the spectrum, children born in wealthy countries, like their parents, consume far more than an equitable share of the world's resources, so even though these children live and thrive, their consumption eliminates the survival chances of thousands of children in the Global South. Whatever one's God may be like, surely His or Her will for children is not mass starvation or death by disease or war.

Myth #3: *All women want to have children.* This notion

is clearly false; there have always been women like myself who have not had maternal inclinations. Among well-known women, the list of non-mothers includes Susan B. Anthony, Simone de Beauvoir, Julia Child, Amelia Earhart, Ella Fitzgerald, Katharine Hepburn, Helen Mirren, Florence Nightingale, Ayn Rand, Diane Sawyer, and Oprah Winfrey, among numerous others. Adoption is an alternative for some women who *do* want to raise children but want to avoid squeezing the planet's resources any further than necessary.

Myth #4: *Having a large number of children and grandchildren is always desirable and a source of pride, and indicates the parents are large-hearted and self-sacrificing.* We've already seen that unrestricted reproduction is not desirable. It therefore cannot be a source of pride, taking resources for one's own surplus children away from children in other countries. True large-heartedness would be to think of what's best for the whole planet, instead of just wanting more cute kiddies who resemble oneself. I've known older women who feel deprived and jealous because they don't have as many grandchildren as their friends do! Population education is an urgent need for both parents and grandparents.

Myth #5: *Adults who deliberately remain childless are selfish and hate children.* Without children, adults can spend their time and energy developing their talents and ways of giving service. Even if they dissipate their resources, their childlessness still benefits the planet and every creature on it.

The notion that the childless hate children has perhaps been encouraged by some websites put up by and for non-parents that rant about how disgusting children are. In my own experience, I've never run into a hatred of children among childless adults. In fact, some have chosen livelihoods, or spend volunteer time, either working directly with children or making life better for them in some way.

Myth #6: *Childless adults are to be pitied.* This myth was expressed in a conversation I overheard between two coworkers in which one said, "I don't understand couples who don't have children. It would be so lonely, and what would they do with their time?" This notion comes perhaps from the assumption that since supposedly all women want children (see Myth #3 above), any woman who doesn't have any must have been unable to have them. Whether a childless woman did or didn't want to have children, pity is a completely inappropriate and offensive response. The woman who didn't want children is happy not to have them. The woman who did want them can be encouraged to grieve her loss, then to explore other options. She may want to bring children into her life by adoption, by moving closer to family or friends who have young children, or by taking up a career that involves working with children. The woman may choose to move on and live fully without children. We can all broaden our thinking to realize more fully that those who live in our household or to whom we are biologically related are not our only family. "The problem with the world," said Mother Teresa, "is that we draw the circle of our family too small."

Myth #7: *Those who don't have children will be abandoned in their old age.* The absurdity of this notion is easily realized by how many elders who have *had* children have been abandoned. Their phones may not ring for weeks. Months may pass between visits, and in the case of adult children who live hundreds of miles away, visits may only be possible once a year or less often. Some adult children living at a distance may need to hire caregivers to care for their parents; others cannot or do not provide financial support to their parents. Now many elders live with other elders in senior living housing, so in these cases there is little difference whether an elder had children or not.

When I was a child, my parents, my brother and I lived with my widowed maternal grandmother in her two-bedroom home. She died when I was eight. Except during her final illness, she assisted ably with cooking, cleaning, laundry and childcare, an immeasurable help to my parents, who both worked outside the home. Because my grandmother's house was paid for, my parents did not have to make a monthly rent or mortgage payment, and could save for our future college expenses. Our grandmother's presence and the stories she told enriched our lives, giving us children a perspective on another generation and the challenges they faced. It is unfortunate that so few children, and their overworked parents, have the additional love and extra pair of hands that a grandparent in the home can provide. It would be even easier to manage today, now that the average home is much larger than the one I lived in. However, now that elders in America—even elders who have had families—do not usually spend their final years living in the homes of relatives, we as a society will need to develop ways to extend community support and needed services to elders. In this way, the fear of being abandoned in old age will not serve as a reason to reproduce.

Myth #8: Children are needed as replacements for their parents. To begin with, we've already seen that the last thing our planet needs is for everyone to replace themselves. However, let's look at the argument at face value. It's true that children do replace parents eventually, with "eventually" being farther into the future than most people realize. Longevity statistics show that the average length of time when *both* the parents and their children are alive, and thus the time period when resources necessary for the child *add* to those of the parent rather than replacing them, is fifty years! That is, a parent today who gives birth at age twenty-five is likely to live to age seventy-five or longer, and thus will probably be alive for at least fifty of the same years that her child is alive. Furthermore, during the first half of these fifty years, there will probably be a grandparent or two alive as well, also consuming resources. This is a substantial change from the situation in former times, when the parent and grandparent's life expectancies were much lower, and infant mortality considerably higher. Furthermore, the duplicated and triplicated resource consumption will be much higher for an American child than for a child in the Global South, as we've already noted.

Although most people consider their children to be a primary source of joy, research reported by Harvard psychology professor Dr. Daniel Gilbert in his fascinating book *Stumbling on Happiness* tells a different story.[9] In four separate studies, married people of different ages were asked to rate their marital happiness at their present stage of life. When these results were compiled, all four studies showed high satisfaction at the beginning of a marriage before there were children, then a sharp dive when children are young. The happiness graph goes up a little after the children are in school, but takes an even sharper dive during the kids' teen years. Only after the last child has left home do their parents report levels of marital satisfaction equal to what they felt before the children were born. Other studies by other researchers show similar findings: parents reported their marriages were happiest before the children were born and after the children left home. Couples without children tended to be the happiest.[10]

In addition, Dr. Gilbert reports on careful studies that

have been done to assess the happiness women experience in doing a variety of household tasks, including those necessary for child care. These studies show that women "are less happy when taking care of the children than when eating, exercising, shopping, napping, or watching television. Indeed, looking after the kids appears to be only slightly more pleasant than doing housework."

There's also the not insignificant matter of money. According to government data, a middle-income family with a child born in 2006 will spend, on average, $197,700 to raise him or her from birth through age seventeen. And this figure doesn't even include the ever-increasing costs of college.[11]

So if continuing to reproduce carelessly threatens life on the planet for everyone, and if parents themselves are not particularly happy in caring for children, why does childbearing still seem to be an unquestioned positive value? Dr. Gilbert explains that if a particular belief has some property that facilitates its own transmission, that belief tends to be held by an increasing number of people. We can easily understand this if the belief is accurate, but why is an inaccurate belief, such as equating children with happiness, so readily transmitted? "False beliefs that promote stable societies," he writes, "tend to propagate because people who hold these beliefs tend to live in stable societies, which provide the means by which false beliefs propagate."[12]

From the time of the first humans until perhaps the

beginning of the twentieth century, it was undoubtedly true that encouraging everyone to have children was necessary for stability and continuity of societies. Now, due to the burdening of our planet and its wildlife with too many humans, this longstanding paradigm has been overturned: now stability and even our survival itself depend on a substantial *reduction* in reproduction. Instead of encouraging and rewarding reproduction, we need to discourage it and make it more costly.

Most of us don't want everyone to stop reproducing, but we needn't worry. Barring massive worldwide epidemics or nuclear war, there will always be enough people having children to ensure that the human race continues. The practical action we must take, if we truly want a reduction in starvation and resource wars, is to help people understand that child rearing is no guarantee of happiness; that in fact it involves long hours of monotonous work, expense, worry and frustration.

We must be careful, however, not to discourage people to rear responsibly the children they already have; all children who are already here deserve their parents' and society's love and support. But to adults who are childless, and those who already have one or two children and want another, we can gently try to communicate the magnitude of the responsibility they are considering and of the world situation, both as regards overpopulation and resource depletion. We can tactfully help young parents understand that having additional children endangers the future survival of their existing children as well as millions of other children around the world. Those who love children can best express that love, paradoxically, by having fewer of them. We can speak up when we hear the myths of pronatalism expressed as unquestioned truth. If potential parents can stand back from our society's urging to have babies long enough to consider the prospect of parenthood clearly, it will be easier for more of them to make the decision not to reproduce.

There are signs that the message is being heard. According to Sylvia Ann Hewlett, author of *The Baby Panic*, currently twenty percent of all U.S. women over age forty are childless, a rate that has doubled in just twenty years. Some may view this statistic negatively, but its benefit to children already born, and to all life on our planet, is clear.

In summary: simple living by Americans could make a major difference in resources freed up to be shared among the billions of humans already on the planet. These resources would contribute directly to world peace by making it less likely that impoverished peoples would resort to violence to get what they need. But it will not be enough unless we can also lower our worldwide birth rate, something every peace-loving potential parent needs to consider very carefully. Once we commit ourselves to speak and write more clearly about what parenting actually involves, and about the urgency of reducing overpopulation, and perhaps to lobby our legislators to establish financial penalties for conceiving children, the average person's choice to limit reproduction will become easier.

Chapter Twelve

War, Terrorism, and Crime

Okay, you may say, I'll bite. How can anything I could do have an effect on wars around the globe, bombs on planes or in subways, or gang activity in our inner cities? We must begin by looking at why people resort to violence.

Causes of violence and war include chauvinism, which is the aggressive patriotism that may lead a ruler or nation to dream of empire, and religious or racial hatreds. These are forms of the belief in group superiority. Wars may begin due to the pressures of overpopulation. Suggestions for dealing with each of these are discussed in earlier chapters.

Here we will take a look at violence arising out of unequal distribution of wealth, which may be instigated either by the poor or by the rich. In the first instance, the poor feel they have no way to fulfill basic needs such as food, shelter, health care, safety or employment; and that their concerns have been repeatedly and consistently marginalized and ignored by those in power. The French Revolution is a well-known example of peasants, desperately needy yet heavily taxed to support the extravagant lifestyle of the rich, finally resorting to violence. Such circumstances occur when the gap between the haves and the have-nots is wide and getting wider. The have-nots are ignored and denied the means of supplying their needs because the haves always want more, even though they have far more than they need already. Indulging in excess consumption is addictive, suppressing the natural feelings of compassion that every human has.

Such greed can lead, on the other hand, to wars begun by rich and powerful government leaders for their own profit and that of their wealthy friends. Rulers intent on maximizing wealth and power first convince their people that there is an enemy nation they must fight in order to protect their safety and security. If there is no enemy, the warmongers are not above inventing one, as George W. Bush did to sell his invasion of Iraq in 2003. His case to Congress and the American people as to why this war was necessary turned out to be completely and knowingly false. "Terrorism is the war of the poor," said Sir Peter Ustinov, "and war is the terrorism of the rich."

Most of us Americans probably think of ourselves as middle class, even perhaps struggling to meet our monthly bills. Like it or not, however, we are all, by world standards, perceived as the haves, and especially greedy haves at that. The percentages of resources we consume are wildly out of proportion to our population, and our demands have no end.

We have multiple choices of cornflakes, own more than one car per person, and waste tons of food every day, while over a billion people worldwide live on less than $1 per day and thousands of children starve. In the Global South, people see us fly into their countries as tourists, stay in luxurious (to them, though perhaps average to us) hotels, and spend more money in a week than they could earn in many years. When I visited Tibet some years ago, our guide told us that when we took out money to buy something in the marketplace, not to show the entire contents of our wallets. To us we had just what we needed to cover our expenses and a few souvenirs, but to local people it was unimaginable riches.

How can our wealth not provoke jealousy and anger among those who work so hard but have no way out of grinding poverty? To make matters worse, we are often arrogant as a nation, behaving as though the American way of life is the best and everyone should live wastefully like we do. We proceed to enforce our policies wherever we want, and wage war anywhere it serves our interests. Why was there so much surprise, in the aftermath of 9/11, that we are hated as much as we are?

It's clear that if we want peace, the gap between the haves and have-nots must be narrowed, and narrowed substantially. We must stop treating the workers of the Global South as our slaves. We've manipulated the world economy so that poor countries must produce luxury goods for the American market, while in truth we need to let them have their own land back for their own sustenance. We must stop the cutting down of tropical forests to make grazing lands for our health-destroying meat habit. Such lands are useless for any purpose within a few years, and more forest land must then be destroyed to continue cattle production. These forests, essential to the wellbeing of the entire planet, are, by some estimates, at a level of destruction so serious they may not be able to recover.[1] We must stop demanding that we can have any food from anywhere on earth any time of the year. We must stop using pesticides that sicken workers in the Global South so that we can satisfy our whims; for example, in the growing of fresh flowers in South America to be shipped to U.S. markets.

The inequity occurs not only internationally, but within our own country as well. According to the Federal Bureau of Labor Statistics, the hourly wage of the average American non-supervisory worker is actually lower, adjusted for inflation, than it was in 1970. Meanwhile, CEO pay has soared—from less than thirty times the average wage to almost 300 times the typical worker's pay!

Now that the U.S. must import most of the oil it uses, partly from the volatile Middle East, we need to reduce our usage drastically. Doing so will lessen the pressure to wage war in that region, which has, in the last five years, killed thousands of American youth and hundreds of thousands of

Middle Eastern people, and destroyed their towns and cities. To reduce our usage, we can implement the suggestions given in the chapter on the environment. We urgently need to put major funding into solar, wind and other alternative energy sources. We can do this through investment choices and by voting for ballot proposals on energy conservation. In addition to preventing war, reducing our fossil fuel usage will address the frightening buildup of greenhouse gases and prepare us for "peak oil," the decline of recoverable oil supplies, which has either already begun or will occur in the very near future. In short, if we want peace, we must reduce our wants to what can be sustainably produced without causing death, destruction, illness and poverty in the Global South.

The fundamentalist Islamic religious beliefs of many terrorists may be repugnant to a largely Christian United States, although a commitment to kill unbelievers has not been a foreign concept in Christianity either, as happened in the Crusades and the Inquisition. History also includes instances of one Christian group at war with another Christian group; e.g., the destruction of the Cathars in the thirteenth century, and in our own lifetime, continuing violence in Northern Ireland. Intolerance and blind adherence to dogma is thus the enemy, not each other.

We can also find a common enemy in corruption, conspicuous consumption and waste, and thus recognize ourselves in Islamic leaders' depiction of Western (especially

American) society as decadent. Do we in the United States really want a society in which our teenage girls dress in ways that suggest they are sexually available, our youth listen to music lyrics that advocate violence and objectification of women, and we overeat ourselves into gross obesity? That's the society we have. We cannot sit down with friends to dinner without being interrupted by a telephone solicitor calling. We've turned shopping into a hobby, and have accumulated so much stuff we have to rent storage units, in addition to our already large houses, in order to store it. When a small appliance stops working, an appliance a person in the Global South would be thrilled to own, we don't repair it; we throw it in the landfill. Can we understand why we look decadent to the rest of the world? Wouldn't we not only defuse violence but make ourselves much happier if we found ways to address our breakdown of personal and societal propriety? I'm not suggesting censorship of any kind, but enough self-awareness to refuse as individuals to support those customs, buying habits, or forms of entertainment that diminish our humanity.

Turning our attention to crime, simple living can reduce violence and destruction here at home as well. By reducing our wants, we will evolve toward needing less income. The gap between the salaries of CEOs and average workers can be decreased, so that there would no longer be a few people earning outrageously high salaries and many others unemployed or underemployed. Why is there no embarrassment on the part of those who flaunt excessive wealth while poverty takes countless lives every day? Why do the rest of us continue to idolize these people in the popular media, even when they behave like spoiled brats or worse? In our everyday conversations, we can question why celebrities are admired, whether it is an accurate assumption that being a millionaire will make us happy, and so on. As the mystique is consciously removed, and conspicuous consumption comes to be viewed as causing widespread suffering, such consumption is likely to decrease. Gradually, envy of the rich by the poor, a clear cause of violence, would decrease as well. Needing less income, parents could spend more time with their children, which would reduce isolation and drug use among youth, high risk factors for crime. If children get attention and feel loved because their parent(s) can be at home with them, they will not be as likely to need violence to establish their self-worth, such as through gang activity. When anger does arise, the youth from strong, caring families will not find it so easy to depersonalize a potential victim. As crime rates drop, we'll be able to reduce public expenditure to build and maintain prisons and support their inmates.

Reducing our "addiction to foreign oil," as former President Bush called it, would positively affect domestic crime as well as war abroad. If wars to secure fossil fuel resources are no longer needed, young people will not be thrown into despair, facing the prospect of senseless injury and death as soldiers. Some who have served as soldiers and had to kill others for no apparent reason may be more likely to resort to crime when they return home. Most will have to deal with the discouragement and possibly even depression resulting from trying to find their place in a society that found them completely expendable in a war based on lies.

In a society of reduced wants, there would be more small, affordable homes available, reducing the number of slums that breed crime. With less income needed, people could work fewer hours and be at home more, better able to notice something amiss in the neighborhood and thus prevent crime before it happens.

Furthermore, in a society of reduced wants, people have more disposable income, more of which can be given to charity. This is no small point: philosopher Peter Singer believes that if people in the rich Western countries would give just one percent of their incomes to hunger relief organizations, poverty and food shortages could be eradicated worldwide.[2] One percent—that's $400 on an annual income of $40,000— seems doable; yet how many people, consuming beyond their means, have enough money left over to be able to give this much?

In summary, if we want to reduce war, terrorism and crime, resorting to more violence is not a sane or effective method to use. As practical peacemakers, we need to remove the causes of violence. These causes are: 1) the unconscionable inequity between the superrich and the desperately poor, which we address by reining in our wants to be closer to our needs. We can also help shift social attitudes toward the superrich away from adulation to embarrassment; 2) the inability of people in the Global South to supply their own needs, which we alleviate by reduced American demands for luxury goods and by increased charitable giving; 3) Americans' addiction to fossil fuel, which we overcome by becoming more fuel efficient in our own lives and by supporting aggressive funding of alternative fuel development; 4) the perception that Americans are decadent and exercise a corrupting influence on the rest of the world, which we defuse by returning to values of frugality, modesty, courtesy, and the support of life- and community-enhancing entertainment; and 5) the alienation of at-risk youth, which we eliminate by creating an income structure that allows working parents to stay home more, which increases affordable housing and lowers the expectation that having lots of expensive toys is an entitlement, or even desirable.

Does What I Do Make a Difference?

"Changing my life takes tedious effort and patience," you may be saying. "Do I really want to work this hard on myself? Those who may benefit are mostly people I'll never meet, and I'm not sure that what I do will make a difference anyway." Let's look at these three points individually.

First, of course it is hard work to change longstanding behavior patterns and to simplify our lives. We fear we will feel deprived without our toys and activity-filled lives. Yet countless people down through the centuries as well as our contemporaries, from founders of major religions to just ordinary folks, testify that these changes bring deep satisfaction and a sense of the sacred into our lives. I am much happier living simply, and I invite readers to continue refining their own lives. The focus we develop by reducing our stuff, our improved health, and the free time we gain will make possible new directions beyond what we may even have dreamed for our lives.

We wonder why we should work on behalf of people

we'll never meet, who may live on the other side of the world, from whom we are divided by profound linguistic and cultural differences. Archeologists tell us, however, that our ancestors may all have originated in Africa. If we share ancestors, that is likely to mean that we are still literally—biologically—related, even after all these millennia, and that we can therefore quite accurately consider ourselves cousins, albeit many times removed. Looking at it this way, are we really so separate from people in other countries? Or are they just members of our family we haven't personally met? Is it easier to cut back our consumption if we believe we are doing it for our cousins instead of for strangers? We also, of course, are doing it for people we know very well: ourselves, our neighbors and family members.

Perhaps the most frequent objection to personal lifestyle change is: What difference can I possibly make? We see the magnitude of the obstacles to peace, the difficulty of changing longstanding habits whether in ourselves or in others, and feel powerless. This sense of futility was tenacious and consistently discouraging for me over a number of years, but I have come to see a number of ways in which each individual does make a difference, regardless of any observable result. Let's examine those ways in detail, first considering the process of how an individual action radiates outward.

Every individual action sets an example. Each time you speak or act, you are demonstrating a way to respond to something life is presenting. You are making hundreds of small choices each day, mostly out of habit, that determine patterns for your own future and for those who observe you. With each choice you are declaring, "This is how I am showing up in my life and in the world."

Every individual example influences others. Those around you note, often unconsciously, what you say and do. If your speech or action relates to an area of life they've been struggling with, they are likely to be extremely attentive to see how you handle it. For example, someone with food addiction tendencies watches you being tempted to overeat junk food at a party, but stopping after minimal indulgence. Someone prone to outbursts of temper sees you provoked to the point of anger but reacting calmly instead. Others—not only those you know well, but also people who are strangers or even who disagree with you—may be paying closer attention to your actions than their outward appearance would suggest. The influence of your choices on others increases the likelihood they will make a similar choice in similar circumstances. Their choices have a direct effect on the habit patterns they are establishing or reinforcing in their own lives, and thus on the suffering they cause or avoid causing.

Once we understand that we are influencing others with our choices, we are more strongly motivated to make those choices positive. We are constantly influencing others, moment by moment, day in and day out. We may see little or no evidence that anyone notices what we do in terms of commenting about our opinions or actions, or changing their own behavior. It has been said that in order to accept a new idea and change one's behavior in accord with it, one must hear an idea at least seven times from different sources. In my experience, seven may not be enough. For example, one may need to hear the numerous health, ethical and environmental reasons to stop eating meat many times before actually reducing one's meat eating even a little. If no one seems to pay attention to what you eat or the kind of vehicle you drive, don't despair; your action counts as one more time someone is being exposed to the new idea. In every case you can at least know that you aren't lending any of your energy to strengthening the opposite tendency to be cruel or wasteful.

When people do imitate a positive example, it strengthens the whole community. Perhaps it is stating the obvious to say that individual actions shape and determine what community expectations and standards will be. We may not think about this very much, because we are not encouraged in our society to regard ourselves as being important unless we are rich or famous. However, any time someone pushes the boundaries of acceptable behavior toward rudeness or deception, that person makes it more likely that others will repeat that action, and it will eventually gain social approval. On the positive side, whenever we act with a more selfless response than might be the norm, such as forgiveness in the face of insult (Jesus' "turning the other cheek"), or compassion to those outside our usual sphere of caring, or refraining from eating or wearing something that has caused either suffering to humans or animals or the degradation of the environment, we create the kind of community that will be life-enhancing, stable, and supportive.

Your positive actions go beyond those who directly benefit, filtering down to others as well. Let's return to our example of refraining from anger. Perhaps someone at work is unkind to you, even insulting, but you respond with forbearance instead of anger. A coworker sees your response and later, finding a stressful situation at home, also refrains from anger. The coworker's spouse and children are direct beneficiaries of your calm response. On the other hand, were you in the habit of giving way to anger, your coworker would have been more likely to blow up at his or her family, speaking or acting in ways that would hurt them. Every time you act responsibly, it has a ripple effect, and the whole community benefits.

Here are some specific areas that are likely to improve as a result of an individual's compassionate actions:

Compassionate actions can lead to stronger relationships and better health. Who doesn't want to be around a positive person? When you develop a habit of compassionate action, you draw people to you. Everyone wants to be valued and treated well. Many people want to overcome their own negative behaviors, and when they see you being positive, they want to hang around to see how you do it. This attraction may not be conscious on their part, but it means you will have more friendship in your own life, and you will strengthen relationships between others. When you act from your highest impulse, stress and anxiety are diminished. You are less likely to hold absolute, polarizing views. You develop sufficient discipline to take better care of yourself, to exercise and to eat moderately and healthfully. If you are not caught up in debt, vengeance or deception, you will probably sleep better. All these factors maximize good health and, as they do, you have more energy to work productively and reach out to help your community.

Compassionate actions can save animals and the planet. Not taking more than we need means our ecological footprint will be smaller. The land that an overconsuming person requires for livestock agriculture, a large home and possibly a vacation home, access for wilderness-destroying recreation and similar pursuits, could be returned to being wildlife habitat. Even if no one else sees what you do, you are still conserving resources.

Several years ago I heard a talk by environmental activist Julia Butterfly Hill, who had sacrificed her comfort and even risked death to live for nearly two years in a giant redwood tree. She was attempting to save a section of old-growth forest from being destroyed. In her talk she tried to raise awareness of paper usage, such as disposable coffee cups, paper towels and toilet paper, noting that even environmental activists typically bring to their meetings coffee in single-use paper cups. Every disposable paper item was once part of a living tree, she reminded the audience. Her passion to preserve trees impressed me deeply and I changed my behavior right away. No one may see me refrain from taking a paper towel when I wash my hands in a public restroom, and certainly no one sees that I am using far less toilet paper than I used to, but it is still saving trees.

Compassionate actions can help those who are discouraged or depressed. The number of Americans seeking medical help for depression is up sharply. According to a Centers for Disease Control and Prevention (CDC) study, adult use of antidepressants almost tripled between 1988–1994 and 1999–2000.[1] A calm and compassionate person can help defuse others' depression by addressing its source. Is the depression cause by money worries? The peacemaker can quietly model frugality. Is the cause unhappy family relationships? The peacemaker can model conflict resolution without anger, sarcasm, manipulation or withdrawal. Is the cause loneliness or isolation? The peacemaker's community-building efforts can provide a support system. Is this going to completely eliminate the problem of depression? No, but it is clearly helpful, and can make a huge difference to a person who is receptive.

When people who are suffering from loss, illness or

mental instability encounter someone calm and kind, they feel better. When we go out of our way to help a person who, unbeknownst to us, may be suicidal, it could save a life. That person feels a ray of hope that maybe life is worth living after all. In order to have this kind of influence, we must be stable and disciplined ourselves. This arises naturally from a committed prayer or mindfulness practice of some kind. Taking time every day for our practice not only helps us, but all those we meet. Collectively, we create a more harmonious society.

Compassionate actions can minimize the incidence of lawbreaking. When a group of peacemakers withdraw from greed and overconsumption, it creates a community of more equal wealth distribution. The more people who live simply, the more resources are available, the more individuals can give to support social services and inner city schools, and the more we can insure that low-income children will have what they need. The percentage of children living below the poverty line has soared in recent years, as has our prison population. For each person who turns away from our society's incessant urging to accumulate more, and instead lives from a compassionate heart, the more the causes of poverty-related crime will be reduced.

If we are honest, courteous and reliable in our dealings, keep our neighborhoods looking neat and clean, do not indulge in conspicuous consumption, and pay attention to each other, chances are that folks who are borderline lawbreakers may, over time, learn to make less destructive choices. For example, if someone hears or observes that many people cheat on their income taxes, that person is more likely to cheat. If a driver sees a number of people speeding and running red lights, s/he is more likely to do likewise. The reverse is also true; it all goes back to the examples we set. I am not speaking here of conscientious lawbreaking to protest unjust laws, which arises from another motivation entirely.

Compassionate actions can show our gratitude. People like to be recognized for the helpful things they do, especially if their actions require extra time and effort. When we express appreciation to someone, that makes it more likely that the person will feel motivated to assist someone else in the future. If we develop gratitude for the unseen labor involved in growing and bringing our food to market, and for all the other kinds of services we enjoy, it makes us less picky and cranky about wanting things just so, and being upset when they're not. This makes us more congenial to live with. It may also incline us to stop short of overindulgence in our eating and drinking. If we are grateful for the presence of family members and friends, are we not less likely to feel anger toward them when they do something that displeases us? It may not look like our gratitude changes anything, but greater harmony will subtly be established, showing us the difference that one person can make in the world.

Our trustworthiness can encourage risk-taking in others.
Every society needs people to challenge the status quo if
we are ever going to evolve toward more peaceful ways of
living. When a community includes a significant number
of people who live simply and sanely, with compassionate
intention to do the least harm possible, and who have the
time and interest to be supportive, community members feel
safer taking risks and expressing their gifts more fully. The
risks may include calmly and non-threateningly bringing up
controversial topics in conversation, and the willingness to
stand alone, if necessary, for causes that may be ridiculed.
Some of us will feel called to speak truth to power, and
possibly engage in civil disobedience when cruel laws
perpetuate injustice. Each ordinary person's trustworthiness
enhances societal evolution at the same time it builds a sense
of one's own value in that society.

*Over time, our compassionate actions make us feel that
our life is worthwhile.* In a society such as ours in which
celebrity is overhyped—even when celebrities' behavior
is shallow or destructive—and in which everyday virtue is
rarely recognized, it is easy to feel that unless a person is
outstanding, s/he is nothing. However, if we determine to live
our lives committed to compassionate service and to setting
positive examples, we will be able to look back over our
lifetime and see how much our time here has mattered. This
will be true even if the surface appearance of our life has

been what society would consider ordinary or even boring. So many people search for meaning, not realizing how much their small daily choices matter. An elder can look back on a life filled with compassionate action and, regardless of how many unskillful choices were made, know that his or her lifetime on earth was a positive influence.

This was brought home to me in considering the work that I do. In the past, when I have looked at my reference librarian position, which I enjoy most of the time, I used to see it as largely unremarkable. I have thought that if I weren't doing it, someone else would take the job; so what did my work matter, even though I did the job well? Then I began to think about how many people I serve every day, answering their questions, and how often they thank me and say they wouldn't have been able to figure out what they needed to know without me. I calculated that during the twelve years I have held my present job, I have helped people over 100,000 times. Following this line of thought, I came to value my contribution more highly. Have you considered your work in the light of how many people you have served, of the sum total of the kindness you have expressed into the world?

Ultimately, we can see that *acting ethically and compassionately reduces other people's suffering, or at least avoids adding to it.* We've noted above several ways in which acting ethically reduces our own suffering: it contributes to good health, solid relationships, a supportive community, and the feeling that our lives are worthwhile. These actions minimize suffering in others as well. If we treat people, animals and the earth with care, content ourselves with simple living and do not take more than our share, take care to avoid irresponsible sexual expression, speak kindly and truthfully, and steer clear of intoxicants, we have made a powerful contribution to others' wellbeing. If we think for a moment how much pain one person can inflict by violating these precepts, we can more clearly see the benefit of each individual who keeps them.

In our daily routine we may lose sight of how important individual actions are in the larger scheme of things. Mahatma Gandhi said that whatever one does will be insignificant, but it is very important that one does it. I interpret this to mean that one's individual actions leading to peace may seem insignificant, but one's intention, commitment and example strengthen others, with whom collectively we can all become peacemakers.

In his essay *The Star Thrower*, the late ecologist Loren Eiseley recalls roaming along a beach in the early morning, observing the struggle to survive shared by all shoreline creatures.[2] "Along the strip of wet sand that marks the ebbing and flowing of the tide," he writes, "death walks hugely and in many forms." Those creatures exposed when the tide goes out will be caught by predators, die of dehydration, or be collected by humans to be boiled—alive, in some cases—

for food. Likewise death walks hugely in our own world, in the forms of species extinction, climate change, habitat destruction, epidemics, starvation, and war.

Eiseley sees a human figure in the distance and walks in that direction. As he draws near, he sees the other man stoop to pick up a starfish. Eiseley asks, "Do you collect?" Throwing it back into the sea, the man replies, "Only like this. Only for the living." Eiseley walks on, then turns back and sees him tossing another starfish back into the surf. In the early morning light, the other man seemed to have "the posture of a god."

Deeply impressed by what the man was doing, Eiseley thinks about it for a long time, pondering humans' capacity for compassion. He realizes how much he cares for these struggling creatures: "I *do* love the world. I love its small ones, the things beaten in the strangling surf, the bird, singing, which flies and falls and is not seen again. . . . I love the lost ones, the failures of the world."

He goes out to find the star thrower once again, and this time joins him in returning the creatures to safety. " 'I understand,' I said. 'Call me another thrower.' He is not alone any longer. After us there will be others."

Hoping and praying for peace, or standing in candlelight vigils, is not enough—we must change our thinking and then our actions. May we all develop the attention, patience and commitment to pick up the next starfish, and the next.

Notes

INTRODUCTION: THE THREE ASPECTS OF SIMPLE LIVING

1. Tolstoy, Leo. *Twenty-three Tales*. Translated by L. and A. Maude. London, New York [etc.]: H. Frowde, 1906.

2. Salzberg, Sharon. "I Feel Your Brain." Interview with Daniel Goleman. *Tricycle: The Buddhist Review* 16:2 (Winter 2006).

CHAPTER ONE: CARELESS EATING AND DRINKING

1. "USDA Livestock Slaughter 2007 Summary," March 2007 and "USDA Poultry Slaughter 2007 Summary," February 2007. United States Department of Agriculture, National Agricultural Statics Service. Available through http://www.nass.usda.gov/Publications/catalog.pdf.

2. "United States Soybean Domestic Consumption," Powerpoint file (September 2007). United Soybean Soybean Board. Available at http://www.unitedsoybean.org/Library/RecentLibraryItems.aspx?category=3. See also "Major Crops Grown in the United States." U.S. Environmental Protection Agency. Accessed September 2008 at http://www.epa.gov/oecaagct/ag101/cropmajor.html.

3. Akers, Keith. *The Lost Religion of Jesus*. New York: Lantern Books, 2000.

4. Callahan, Rick. "States Push Online Fitness Programs." Associated Press. MSNBC.com, March 18, 2000. Accessed September 2008 at http://www.msnbc.msn.com/id/17676579/.

5. "USDA Livestock Slaughter 2007 Summary," March 2007 and "USDA poultry Slaughter 2007 summary," February 2007. United States Department of Agriculture.

6. Ornish, Dean. *Love and Survival: The Scientific Basis for the Healing Power of Intimacy*. New York: HarperCollins, 1998.

7. Nhat Hanh, Thich. *Creating True Peace*. Riverside, NJ: Free Press, 2003, p. 77.

CHAPTER TWO: OVERCOMMITTING OUR TIME

1. Dacyczyn, Amy. *The Complete Tightwad Gazette: Promoting Thrift as a Viable Alternative Lifestyle*. New York: Villard Books, 1998.

CHAPTER THREE: INSTANT GRATIFICATION

1. Gyatso, Tenzin (His Holiness the XIV Dalai Lama). *The Art of Living*. London: Thorsons, 2001, p. 11.

2. Angier, Michael. "The Eighth Wonder of the World." Accessed September 2008 at http://www.successnet.org/articles/angier-8thwonder.htm.

3. "United States Economy." Microsoft Encarta Online Encyclopedia 2008. Accessed September 2008 at http://encarta.msn.com.

4. "U.S. Savings Rate Hits Lowest Level Since 1933." Associated Press. MSNBC.com, January 30, 2006. Accessed September 2008 at http://www.msnbc.msn.com/id/11098797.

CHAPTER FOUR: UNEXAMINED OPINIONS

1. Seng-Tsan. *Hsin-Hsin Ming: Verses on the Faith-Mind*. Translated by Richard B. Clarke. Buffalo, NY: White Pine Press, 2001.

2. Katie, Byron. *Loving What Is*. New York: Harmony Books, 2002.

CHAPTER SIX: ADVERTISING WITHOUT ACCOUNTABILITY

1. Governors State University webserve. "Intrusion." Accessed September 2008 at webserve.govst.edu/pa/Advertising/Wrongs/intrusion.htm.

2. Barber, Benjamin. *Con$umed: How Markets Corrupt Children, Infantilize Adults, and Swallow Citizens Whole*. New York: W. W. Norton, 2007.

3. Ibid.

4. Ulaby, Neda. "State-of-the-Art Ads Are Increasingly One-to-One." Broadcast on National Public Radio's *All Things Considered*, May 29, 2007.

5. Ibid.

6. Ruskin, Gary. "A 'Death Spiral of Disrespect'; If the Consumer is Really King, Why Do Marketers Keep Bombarding Him?" Commercial Alert, April 26, 2004. Accessed September 2008 at http://www.commercialalert. org/Yankelovich.pdf.

7. San Francisco Department of the Environment press release, January 26, 2006.

8. Yankelovich Partners poll for the American Association of Advertising Agencies, April 2004. See "Consumer Resistance to Marketing Reaches All-Time High; Marketing Productivity Plummets, According to Yankelovich Study." Accessed September 2008 at www.commercialalert. org/Yankelovich.pdf.

9. Zerbisias, Antonia. "Urging people not to consume is a tough sell." *Toronto Star*, April 17, 2006.

10. Ibid.

CHAPTER SEVEN: MEDIA SATURATION

1. *Jack Myers Media Business Report, a* study conducted online among 4,000 adults and 1,000 teens, reported October 26, 2005. Accessed September 2008 at http://www.mediavillage.com/jmr/2005/10/26/jmr-10-26-05.

CHAPTER EIGHT: RUDENESS

1. Searcey, Dionne. "Oblivious Thumb Typers Hit Walls, Lose Face." *The Wall Street Journal*, July 25, 2008.

2. McFalls, Joseph A., Jr. "What's a Household? What's a Family?" Population Reference Bureau, November 2003. Available at http://www.prb.org/Articles/2003/WhatsaHouseholdWhatsaFamily.aspx.

CHAPTER TEN: ENVIRONMENTAL DEGRADATION

1. "Livestock a major threat to environment; remedies urgently needed." Food and Agriculture Organization of the United Nations, press release, November 29, 2006.

2. See Plane Stupid's facts on air travel and climate change at http://www.planestupid.com/?q=climate.

3. June 16, 1840 journal entry in Thoreau, Henry David, *The Heart of Thoreau's Journals*. Edited by Odell Shepard. New York: Dover Publications, 1961.

CHAPTER ELEVEN: OVERPOPULATION

1. The State of Food Insecurity in the World 2006. Food and Agriculture Organization of the United Nations. Available at http://www.fao.org.

2. Black, Robert, Saul Morris, and Jennifer Bryce. "Where and Why Are 10 Million Children Dying Every Year?" The Lancet 361:9376 (2003), pp. 2226-2234.

3. "US Population to Reach 300 Million by October." *Voice of America News*, July 11, 2006. Available at http://www.voanews.com.

4. Population Connection Fact Sheet, "The Demographic Facts of Life." Spring 2004. See http://www.populationconnection.org.

5. Population Connection Fact Sheet, "Global Warming." Winter 2007.

6. Population Connection Fact Sheet, "Population and the Environment." Created October 2000, updated June 2002.

7. Alan Kuper, quoted in Frosty Wooldridge, "The Next Added 100 Million Americans—Part 28." *BorderFire Report*, April 5, 2007. Accessed September 2008 at http://www.borderfirereport.net/frosty-wooldridge/the-next-added-100-million-americans-part-28.html.

8. Population Connection Fact Sheet, "USA at 300 Million: A Plan for Action." Fall 2006.

9. Gilbert, Daniel. *Stumbling on Happiness*. New York: Vintage, 2005.

10. Studies done by Elmer Spreitzer and Eldon Snyder, working at Bowling Green State University, and by Angus Campbell and colleagues, working at the University of Michigan. Cited in *The Discovery of Happiness*. Edited by Stuart McCready. Naperville, IL: Sourcebooks Inc., 2001.

11. Chu, Kathy. "You and me and baby makes $197,700." *USA Today*, July 19, 2007.

12. Gilbert, Daniel. *Stumbling on Happiness*. New York: Vintage, 2005, p. 217.

CHAPTER TWELVE: WAR, TERRORISM, AND CRIME

1. Schochet, Joy. "Rainforests in Peril: Deforestation," in Tropical Rainforests. Rainforestconservation.org. Accessed September 2008 at http://www.rainforestconservation.org/articles/rainforest_primer/3.html.

2. Singer, Peter. "Extending Generosity to the Wider World," *The Mercury News*, June 30, 2002.

CONCLUSION

1. "Almost Half of Americans Use at Least One Prescription Drug." Centers for Disease Control and Prevention press release, December 2, 2004.

2. Eiseley, Loren. *The Star Thrower*. New York: Times Books, 1978, pp. 169–185.